MEDICINE
WHEELS

Here
You go !!

Hope you enjoy !!!

(White Flower.)
OSINDRA .

MEDICINE WHEELS

Ancient Teachings for Modern Times

ROY I. WILSON

CROSSROAD · NEW YORK

1994
The Crossroad Publishing Company
370 Lexington Avenue, New York, NY 10017

Printed in the United States of America

The Twelve Steps are reprinted with permission of Alcoholics Anonymous World Services, Inc. Permission to reprint this material does not mean that AA has reviewed or approved the contents of this publication, nor that AA agrees with the views expressed herein. AA is a program of recovery from alcoholism—use of the Twelve Steps in connection with programs and activities which are patterned after AA, but which address other problems, does not imply otherwise.

Library of Congress Cataloging-in-Publication Data

Wilson, Roy I.
    Medicine wheels : Ancient teachings for modern times / by Roy
I. Wilson.
        p. cm.
    Includes bibliographical references.
    ISBN 0-8245-1416-5
    1. Spiritual life—New Age movement. 2. Medicine wheels—
Miscellanea. 3. Indians of North America—Rites and ceremonies—
Miscellanea. I. Title.
BP605.N48W557 1994
299'.74—dc20   94–2388
                                                              CIP

Contents

Part III
CIRCLES

Introduction

Christians receive their spiritual directives from a book they call the Bible. Some Indian tribes carved their stories on totem poles, whereas others beaded their laws into belts. Some tribes received visions from the Great Spirit and placed these teachings on sacred shields or with stones on the ground in what many call Medicine Wheels, and which some tribes call Sacred Hoops. Others call them the Wheel of Life. They are the Indian Bible. Native American Indian people receive their spiritual directives from these ancient Medicine Wheels. They are guides to our lives.

There are many Medicine Wheels. The universe is a Medicine Wheel. Our own solar system is a giant Medicine Wheel. The earth is a Medicine Wheel. Every nation is a Medicine Wheel. Each state is a Medicine Wheel. Each family is a Medicine Wheel. You are a Medicine Wheel, for every individual is a Medicine Wheel.

Sometimes wheels break down. They lose spokes or portions of the rim may break away. The hub may grow weak and fail to keep the spokes in alignment. Our Native American Indian tribes were powerful Medicine Wheels before the white man and woman arrived on this continent. Those Medicine Wheels then became badly damaged and lost their strength. The Christian church became the great oppressor to Native American spirituality. Missionaries did much to destroy Native American spirituality with their exclusivist and anthropocentric teachings. But much good has taken place during the last few decades in the mending of these Sacred Hoops. It is my hope that this book may play an important role in the continuation of that mending.

The potential power in everyone's life is much greater than is now being realized. Many people are living broken lives. The Medicine Wheel of their life is in a poor state of being and in need of repair. We should be about the business of mending our Sacred Hoop.

The word *medicine* has a special meaning to Native American people that is quite different from the meaning understood by non-natives. The non-Indian thinks of medicine as something that he or she may pick up at the local pharmacy when having a prescription filled. An Indian may think of cedar, the sacred sage, a feather, or an eagle flying overhead as his or her powerful medicine. All of these items and many others speak of power. If a Native American should walk into a church for the very first time and see the cross above the altar, he or she may not have any idea what it means, but he or she will probably say to himself or herself that this must be powerful medicine to the people who come here. He or she may not understand the meaning of the Eucharist as it is being served to the people, but he or she will be very aware that it is powerful medicine to these people.

Ed McGaa, Eagle Man, an Oglala Sioux, talks about medicine when he tells us about an individual's sacred shield: "A shield reflected the symbology of a warrior's medicine. 'Medicine' to the plains tribes carried a broader scope in its meaning than simple medical healing for physical affliction or injury. Medicine reached into all facets of a person's life. Protection in combat, success in the hunt, success in lovemaking and mate selection, protection from evil doing, and success in visions and dreams were major petitions and were reflected in the symbols found on Sioux shields."[1]

Most of this book looks into the teachings of the sundance in the Medicine Wheel. There is a brief study of the Red Road and Black Road Medicine Wheel. Reference is made to a few other Medicine Wheels.

This book is not intended to be an exhaustive study of the Medicine Wheels. The knowledge that is held by my elders throughout the land is like unto the sands of the seashore. What I know is equal to only one of those grains of sand on the seashore. I am willing to share my grain of sand in the hope that it might bring healing to some who might read this book. It is the intent of this work to be a vehicle of healing: healing for the individual as well as for collective cultural groups; healing for Christians who have been oppressive by thinking that our ways were heathen and pagan; healing for my own people who are caught in the stress of trying to decide between the old traditional ways and those of the dominant culture. It is my prayer that many of my own people will return to their traditional roots, renewing their belief system and restoring their spiritual strength.

My first study in comparative religion, many years ago when I was a seminarian, made the grave mistake of studying the distinctions or differences among the religions of the world. The study, however, becomes a vastly rewarding one when we make it one of seeking similarities among those religions instead of placing emphasis on their differences. I am certain that my experience was very similar to that which was realized in most, if not all, of the seminaries of that time. I am also convinced that the Sacred Mystery (God) has been in the business of revealing the deity's self to all people, in all cultures, through all time. Let me share my grain of sand with you!

The major part of this study allows us to look into the comparisons among three of the world's great spiritualities: Native American spirituality, Ancient Judaism, and Christianity. My aim is to break down many prejudices that prevail among these groups. The approach is simple; the task is great. We begin the study by looking at Judaism and Christianity through the eyes of Native American spirituality as revealed in the Medicine Wheels. A small portion of this study compares the teachings of the Native American Medicine Wheel with those of other religions and cultures of the world, both ancient and contemporary.

A story has been told about an ancient king who sent five men out to find a strange animal and to return and describe it to him. All five of the men were blind. When they returned, the first man told the king that the animal was like a tree trunk. The second said that it was like a tobacco leaf. The third man said it was like a snake, and the fourth said it was like a boulder. The fifth man said that it was like a hose. They were all describing the same animal! What was it? The king unraveled the riddle, and he said that they were all correct in their descriptions. They had met an elephant. One blind man felt its leg and said that it was like a tree trunk, whereas the one who felt the ear said it was like a tobacco leaf. The body was like a boulder, and the tail was like a snake. The elephant's trunk was like a hose.

The people of the religions of the world all sit together in a great Medicine Wheel with the sacred deity at the central altar. All of them have been attempting to describe this deity, and they have been very much like these blind men who were attempting to describe their animal. They are all correct, but they are each limited to their own experiences. Let us attempt to unravel the riddle by listening to all of their experiences. To do so we must show respect to each other.

This is an exciting adventure!

Tom Brown, in talking about walking the spirit road, says,

> The spiritual path is truly the stuff of life. Once rooted on a spiritual path, I found that life loosened its shallow fleshiness, that I was able to transcend time and place, and enter a new, fuller dimension of life. The path of a spiritual seeker is one of the most difficult paths a man or woman can walk in life, and I urge it on no one unwilling to devote the time or take the risks involved. It takes a lifetime to understand and a zealous dedication to reach this higher plane of existence. The spiritual is a world to which the seeker comes slowly—first with the faith of a child and then with the patience and dedication of a sage. It requires one to let go of all beliefs, all prejudices, and all need for scientific methods of verification. One must abandon logical thinking and learn to deal in the abstract, learn to accept that each moment is an eternity and that each entity becomes, at once, a physical and spiritual teacher.[2]

Remember, everything and everyone is a teacher! Become a seeker and walk the path with me. Begin now to mend the Sacred Hoop of your life as you continue to read these pages.

Part I

Medicine Wheels

1

Comparative Visions of the Medicine Wheel

There are many ancient visions of the Medicine Wheel from all over the world. Three of these have some very interesting comparative values. The Native American vision of the Medicine Wheel is very ancient. Its origin is lost in the antiquity of time. John, the beloved disciple of Jesus, had his vision in 96 A.D. while he was on the Isle of Patmos. Ezekiel, a member of those ancient tribal people known as the twelve tribes of Israel, received his vision in 593 B.C.

You may desire to create your own Medicine Wheel on the floor as we read the scriptures together. If so, you need to gather thirty-six stones for the building of your Medicine Wheel.

John the Revelator's Vision

We begin by reading from the Christian scriptures in Chapter 4 of the Book of Revelation. Begin with verse 1:

"After this I looked, and lo, in heaven an open door! And the first voice, which I had heard speaking to me like a trumpet, said, 'Come up hither, and I will show you what must take place after this.' At once I was in the Spirit, and lo, a throne stood in heaven, with one seated on the throne! And he who sat there appeared like jasper and carnelian, and round the throne was a rainbow that looked like an emerald" (RSV). John, the revelator, begins by telling us that he saw an open door in heaven, and upon entering he discovered that he was in heaven's throne room. It is interesting to note that he did not describe heaven's throne as being made out of jasper stone, but that "He who sat there appeared like jasper."

At this point take your largest stone and place it on the floor in the center of the room (see Figure 1).

center stone of circle

Great Spirit, or God

Figure 1.

sacred altar

Your stone may not be jasper, but you can imagine that it is. I use a jasper stone. John says that this is our symbol for God. The stone in the center of the Native American Indian Medicine Wheel is the sacred altar, and the dwelling place of the Great Spirit or the sacred mystery. The sacred altar is also in the center of the sweatlodge. The sweatlodge is a Medicine Wheel of its own kind, and in the center of the lodge is a small pit that we fill with red-hot stones, which is also the sacred altar wherein we find the presence of the Great Spirit or God.

Missionaries told us we were heathen or pagan to speak of these stones as representing God. They thought of us as pantheists. Actually many of us consider ourselves as being *panentheists*, as do many Christians. After we became Christians we were happy to discover that we were not alone in our belief, for John, the beloved of Jesus, must have been heathen and pagan like us, for he also saw the stone as a symbol of God. And why not? What is the oldest element on earth? Is it not stone? What better symbol for the "Ancient of Days" (Daniel), The Eternal One—the Great Spirit or God. Sometimes Christians question why we address God as "Grandfather" in our prayers. They ask, "Why do you not use the term 'Father' as Jesus taught us?" Grandfather, like the stone, is a good symbol of the Elder One. What father can say that he is older than his grandfather? The grandfather (like the stone) is the oldest, and is therefore a better symbol of the Ancient of Days or God.

Previously we mentioned that the stones in the sweatlodge are red hot. Indian people say that the Great Spirit speaks to them out of the fire. Once again, the missionaries declared that this was pagan and heathen, and that we must drop this from our belief system if we were going to become good Christians. But, after we became Christians, we soon discovered that there was a very powerful man in the ancient stories of the Old Testament. His name was Moses, and he also believed that God spoke to him out of the fire. We had not been Christians very long before we discovered that we had two great biblical figures on our side who must have been heathen and pagan like us, John from the New Testament stories and Moses from the Old Testament.

Returning to our Bible reading in Revelation, pick up by reading verse 4 of Chapter 4: "Round the throne were twenty-four thrones, and seated on the thrones were twenty-four elders, clad in white garments, with golden crowns upon their heads" (RSV). John saw twenty-four elders on twenty-four thrones in a circle around the great central throne.

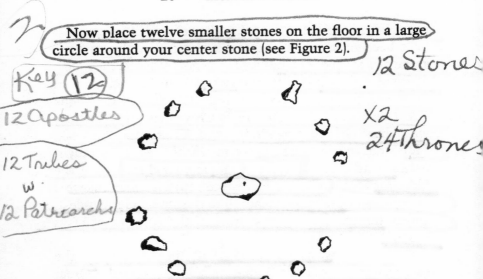

Now place twelve smaller stones on the floor in a large circle around your center stone (see Figure 2).

[handwritten annotations: Key 12, 12 Apostles, 12 Tribes w. 12 Patriarchs, 12 Stones, x2 24 Thrones]

Figure 2.

Your first reaction may be, "Why twelve? John said there were twenty-four." So we must turn to the theologians and ask them who the twenty-four elders are. Many of them will respond by saying that they are the twelve patriarchs of the twelve tribes of ancient Israel in Old Testament Judaism, and the twelve apostles of the New Testament church—two sets of twelve. Twelve is the key number.

On the sacred shields we use black and white feathers instead of stones. Some people call these shields *mandalas.* These feathers then give us twelve blacks and twelve whites in the outer circle (the twenty-four thrones). We will discuss these stones or feathers in a later chapter.

Now read verse 5 of chapter 4 of Revelation: "From the throne issue flashes of lightning, and voices and peals of thunder, and before the throne burn seven torches of fire, which are the seven spirits of God" (RSV) . . . John saw

[handwritten annotations: Key 7, 7 torches of fire, 7 spirits of God, 7 lamps, 7 eyes of God]

flashes of lightning come from the throne in the center—fire!! This is the fire from the stones in the center of the sweatlodge that we spoke of earlier. The voices John heard are those of the Great Spirit—God.

John then saw seven torches of fire in an inner circle immediately around the throne. Some versions say "Seven lamps," and at least one version says "The seven eyes of God." But, regardless of translation, all of the versions say that these seven are "The seven spirits of God." Now it is time for you to take seven more of your stones and place them on the floor in an inner circle immediately around the center stone (see figure 3).

Figure 3.

John said these were the seven spirits of God. Many Native American Indians refer to these seven stones as the seven spirit messengers of the Great Spirit. We further discuss these spirit messengers in a later chapter.

More and more the Medicine Wheel is taking shape on the floor before you with the exact number of stones it had in its pre–European contact form. It is ancient.

Now let us read the balance of the fourth chapter from Revelation beginning at verse 6:

LION
BUFFALO
BEAR
EAGLE

> [A]nd before the throne there is as it were a sea of glass, like crystal. And round the throne, on each side of the throne, are four living creatures, full of eyes in front and behind: the first living creature like a lion, the second living creature like an ox, the third living creature with the face of a man, and the fourth living creature like a flying eagle. And the four living creatures, each of them with six wings, are full of eyes all around and within, and day and night they never cease to sing, "Holy, holy, holy, is the Lord God Almighty, who was and is and is to come!" And whenever the living creatures give glory and honor and thanks to him who is seated on the throne, who lives for ever and ever, the twenty-four elders fall down before him who is seated on the throne and worship him who lives for ever and ever; they cast their crowns before the throne, singing, "Worthy art thou, our Lord and God, to receive glory and honor and power, for thou didst create all things, and by thy will they existed and were created." (RSV)

John saw four living creatures on the four sides of the throne in the outer circle—in the East, the South, the West, and in the North. Now take four stones and place them on the floor in the positions of the four directions. These represent the four winds, the four powers, or the four directions. Whenever we describe either the four directions or the four powers, we are also giving a description of the four winds. The concept of wind adds the idea of spirit to the four directions and the four powers, just as the *Ruach* and the *Pneuma* mean "breath" or "wind" in the ancient Hebrew and Greek languages but are interpreted as speaking of spirit (see figure 4).

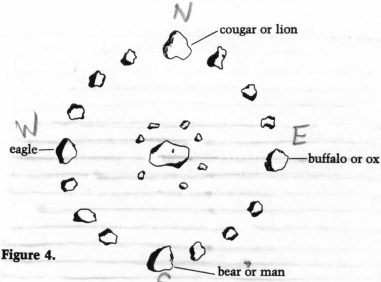

Figure 4.

John saw these as the lion, the ox, man, and the flying eagle. These are the same four as revealed in Ezekiel's vision as you will shortly see. In some of our Indian Medicine Wheels these are the cougar (our North American mountain lion), the buffalo (which can interbreed with the cattle—ox), the bear (a symbol of man, as you will see in a later chapter), and the eagle. The eagle at the sacred altar in the center of the Medicine Wheel is symbolic of the Great Spirit, or God. The eagle in the western direction of the outer wheel of humanity, is God incarnate in all of humanity. All three of these ancient visions have the same symbols.

The Powers of the Four Directions

Previously we saw that the powers of the four directions in the Medicine Wheel are the buffalo, bear, eagle, and cougar, and that these compare to the ox, man, eagle, and lion in the visions of both John and Ezekiel.

Some legends tell us that the Great Spirit had four sons who argued over which one was the most powerful. Didn't Jesus' disciples argue among themselves as to who was the greatest? The Great Spirit then divided the divine powers equally among the four sons. To one was given the power of the East, the power of the buffalo. To another was given the power of the South, the power of the bear. To the third was given the power of the West, the power of the eagle. The fourth son was given the power of the North, the power of the cougar. The Great Spirit told the four sons that they were now co-equal in power, and that they would experience complete power only in unity with each other. What a powerful lesson is here for us, for we are actually talking about the power that lies resident within ourselves. A balanced life comes only by bringing all of the powers of the Medicine Wheel together in one's life. People become out of balance when they concentrate on their own growth in the singular development of one of the powers instead of bringing together a balanced development of all four of the powers within themselves.

For example, when we talk about the animals we are actually talking about people. Therefore, when we talk about the cougar we are talking about cougar people. If you were born as a cougar of the East, a yellow cougar, you may have developed your cougar powers of enlightenment. But, if you never journeyed around to the South and developed your white cougar powers, then your East powers of enlightenment would not be completely utilized in your growth and development. This cougar person needs to journey around to the West also for the development of his or her black cougar self. Otherwise the growth and development of the cougar person's enlightenment may be entirely in the area of perceptions of the outer world about him or her, and be completely neglectful of the growth and development of insights, or enlightenment, regarding the inner self. Therefore, we can see that if we develop our powers in only one direction we are certainly out of balance. We still need to journey around to the North and develop our red cougar self. It is here that we learn how to take all that we have learned about ourselves as cougar people in each of the other directions and apply it to the daily stress of life itself. The Wheel of Life will not turn for us properly when we are out of balance. In fact we can develop our powers in three of the directions, but not in the fourth, and we will still be out of balance.

These four powers are discussed at greater length at the end of each of the four chapters that teach the individual four directional teachings—Chapters 3–6. They are also discussed further in Chapter 7 as we look at their cyclical nature.

As Native American Indian people we see all of the stones in the Medicine Wheel as representatives of the four-leggeds and the wingeds, which in turn are symbolic of spirit beings and two-legged humans. The center stone is the eagle, which is symbolic of God the Great Spirit. The stones in the four directions are the buffalo, bear, eagle, and cougar, which are symbolic of the four powers of the Great Spirit. The seven stones of the inner wheel are the owl, cougar, hawk, coyote, wolf, bear, and raven, which are symbolic of the seven spirit messengers of the Great Spirit. The twelve stones in the outer circle are the snow goose, otter, cougar, hawk, beaver, deer, flicker, sturgeon, bear, raven, snake, and elk, which are symbolic of two-legged human beings.

Now take twelve stones and place three of them in each quarter, lining them up between one of the stones representing the four directions and the center stone. These may appear to look like spokes in a wheel. They are paths from our outer world to the altar of the Great Spirit, or God. Your Medicine Wheel should now look like Figure 5.

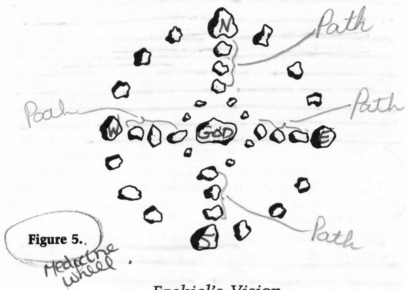

Figure 5.

Ezekiel's Vision

John saw our traditional Native American Medicine Wheel nearly two thousand years ago. Ezekiel saw the same Medicine Wheel nearly seven hundred years before John. We now turn to those non-Christian scriptures of the Old Testament, to the Book of Ezekiel. Non-Christian? Oh, yes, because these are Jewish scriptures that were written long before Christianity was born. These are the scriptures of another religion. This is a vision given to another cultural group of people.

We begin with verse 4 of Chapter 1 of Ezekiel and read through verse 10:

As I looked, behold, a stormy wind came out of the north, and a great cloud, with brightness round about it, and fire flashing forth continually, and in the midst of the fire, as it were gleaming bronze. And from the midst of it came the likeness of four living creatures. And this was their appearance: they had the form of men, but each had four faces, and each of them had four wings. Their legs were straight, and the soles of their feet were like the sole of a calf's foot; and they sparkled like burnished bronze. Under their wings on their four sides they had human hands. And the four had their faces and their wings thus: their wings touched one another; they went every one straight forward, without turning as they went. As for the likeness of their faces, each had the face of a man in front; the four had the face of a lion on the right side, the four had the face of an ox on the left side, and the four had the face of an eagle at the back. (RSV)

How amazing! Ezekiel had a vision of the same four living creatures as did John, and the same as in this Native American Indian Medicine Wheel.

Now read verses 11 through 16:

Such were their faces. And their wings were spread out above; each creature had two wings, each of which touched the wing of another, while two covered their bodies. And each went straight forward; wherever the spirit would go, they went, without turning as they went. In the midst of the living creatures there was something that looked like burning coals of fire, like torches moving to and fro among the living creatures; and the fire was bright, and out of the fire went forth lightning. And the living creatures darted to and fro, like a flash of lightning. Now as I looked at the living creatures, I saw a wheel upon the earth beside the living creatures, one for each of the four of them. As for

chrysolite

the appearance of the wheels and their construction: their appearance was like the gleaming of a chrysolite; and the four had the same likeness, their construction being as it were a wheel within a wheel. (RSV)

Summary

Ezekiel saw both the outer and the inner wheels—"A wheel within a wheel." He also saw the torches or lamps, as well as the fire seen in both John's vision and in the Native American Indian sweatlodge Medicine Wheel. As you continue to read the chapter you notice that Ezekiel also was aware of the importance of the four directions.

John ended his description by saying,"Holy, holy holy," as he gives praise to the creator. We also, as Indian people, could sing "Heleluyan"—our Native American version of the Hallelujah chorus.

This chapter introduces us to a subject of great depth— the Native American Indian Medicine Wheel. A valid question that arises is: Will we continue to see strong parallels or similarities among the teachings of these three great cultural traditions if we should venture into a study of the Native American Indian teachings in the Medicine Wheel? The following chapters lead us into this exciting adventure. We consider circle teachings, teachings of each of the four directions individually, teachings of the four directions collectively or the cycle teachings, and teachings of the seven stones in the inner circle and the twelve in the outer circle. Leave your stones set up in the Medicine Wheel as you continue to read. Save your stones should you discontinue reading so that you may rebuild the Wheel when you begin again. The parallels will continue to intrigue you!

Get Stones for wheel

2

◆◇◆

The Sundance Medicine Wheel

The sun dances around the Earth Mother each day, and in the relationship between the two we learn many of our lessons for life. These lessons are not unlike those that are taught in the Jewish and Christian scriptures as well as in the teachings of many other world religions.

The cycle of the sun around the earth is reflected in the Medicine Wheel. The sun teaches us many lessons in its relationship with the earth. The sun rising in the East teaches us many lessons. The color of this direction is the color of the rising sun—yellow. The sun then dances around to the South, where it reaches its highest point at noontime each day. This is the time of day when it is the clearest and one can see the greatest distance, therefore the color of this direction is white, although in some Medicine Wheels the color of this direction is red, and in others it is green. The sun then dances around to the West, where it sets and brings on the darkness of night. The color of this direction is black. We do not see the sun as it dances around to the North, but we do feel the cold winds from the sunless North. It takes the very stamina and strength of life to face the storms of the North. The color of life is the color of blood—red. This is the color of the North. Some Medicine Wheels make this direction white, but the teachings are all compatible.

We have noticed that there are variations of the use of the colors in the Sundance Medicine Wheel, as shown in the following chart (see figure 6):

	BLACK ELK	HYEMEYOHSTS STORM	SUN BEAR	LAME DEER	SACRED GROUND
NORTH	WHITE	WHITE	WHITE	RED	RED
EAST	RED	YELLOW	YELLOW	YELLOW	YELLOW
SOUTH	YELLOW	GREEN	RED	WHITE	WHITE
WEST	BLACK	BLACK	BLACK	BLACK	BLACK

Figure 6.

A person might ask which of these visions is the correct one. The fundamentalist, exclusivist mind will say that only one of them can be correct. The Native American Indian mind says that they are all correct. All views are valid in a circular theology.

My vision is identical to that of Lame Deer and the multiple writers of the book *Sacred Ground*. This version is used for the basis of this work, but we include all of the teachings of the other versions of this vision to enlarge and enhance our understanding of the teachings of the Sundance Medicine Wheel.

Native spirituality is circular. The Medicine Wheel is a circle. The altar is in the center, and the human race sits in the outer circle. We all have different views of the altar—God. We all see it from different angles. Look at the stones in your Medicine Wheel on the floor. Now sit at the position of one of those stones in the outer circle. Carefully study the stone in the center—the altar. Now move to another position in the outer circle. The center stone looks different to you now, especially if you moved to the diametric opposite side of the Medicine Wheel. The fundamentalist is the static one who never moves around the wheel and believes that his or her view is the only valid view. The eclectic moves freely about the wheel and soon realizes that all of the views are valid ones. All of the visions in the chart are valid. We can learn from each one of them. As we sit in the circle with all of our fellow human creatures, we discover that we have differing views of God and of life. God is reflected through each of us through our own individual experiences. Likewise, all of the variations of the sundance in the Medicine Wheel are valid. The variations in the colors simply provide the richness of different teachings and understandings. The more we can move freely about the wheel, the more balance we find in our spiritual walk and the more spiritual depth we experience in our lives. It can change our worldview by giving us rich new perceptions. Let us listen to some of these teachers.

Black Elk, when speaking of the sacred pipe, said,

> These four ribbons hanging here on the stem are the four quarters of the universe. The black one is for the west where the thunder beings live to send us rain; the white one for the north, whence comes the great white cleansing wind; the red one for the east, whence springs the light and where the morning star lives to give men wisdom; the yellow for the south whence come the summer and the power to grow.
>
> But these four spirits are only one spirit after all, and this eagle feather here is for that one, which is like a father.[1]

Lame Deer says,

> Black represents the west; red, the north; yellow, the east; white, the south. Black is night, darkness, mys-

tery, the sun that has gone down. Red is the earth, the pipestone, the blood of the people. Yellow is the sun as it rises in the east to light the world. White is the glare of the sun as it reaches its zenith. Red, white, black, yellow—these are the true colors. They give us the four directions; you might also say a trail toward our prayers. One reason we are so fascinated with these colors is that they stand for the unity of man—for the black race, the scarlet race, the yellow race, the white race as our brothers and sisters.[2]

In Hyemeyohsts Storm's Medicine Wheel we find, "The north is white, the east is yellow, the south is green, the west is black."[3]

Sun Bear reveals that his vision gives him colors for the twelve directions—the twelve moons. His primary colors are: white in the North, yellow in the East, red in the South, and black in the West.

The writers of *Sacred Ground*[4] give the same colors as Lame Deer, and these are also the colors of my vision.

Let us now go back to the chart. All of the visions agree that the West is black, and they teach similar lessons.

Three have given the North as white and two have revealed the color as red. There is no conflict. White reminds us of the snow that comes out of the North and the winter winds that bring our storms. It also reminds us of the white hairs of our elders. We discover in greater detail that this is the direction that gives us our teachings of the elders in Chapter 7 as we study the life cycle. Red reminds us of the blood of the people—life. It takes the very strength of life to face the storms, whether they be physical, sociological, psychological, philosophical, spiritual, or otherwise. Both colors are valid and interface in the same teachings.

Four of the teachers have given the East as yellow and one as red, but they all are speaking of the rising sun as it begins its sundance in the East and begins dancing toward the South and its setting in the West.

The direction with the greatest seeming discrepancy is the South, but there is no real discrepancy. Yellow, white, and red are all speaking of the sun as it dances in the South—its highest point. Yellow and red speak of its warmth in the South, and white speaks of its glare and the fact that this is the time of day when we can see the greatest distance. Green speaks of the growth that Mother Earth gives to all plant life when Grandfather Sun reaches its zenith, its highest point in the sky, thus penetrating Mother Earth with extra life-giving forces.

All of the Medicine Wheels interface as they also sit in the outer circle of the great Medicine Wheel (see Figure 7).

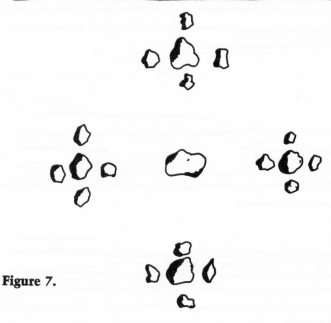

Figure 7.

It is in listening to all of them that we receive the culmination of the teachings. Likewise, let us recognize that all

of the world's spiritual teachings interface in the great circle of the Medicine Wheel. Native American spirituality, Judaism, Christianity, Buddhism, Islam, and all of the other world religions are the outer circle of the Medicine Wheel. To refuse to consider all of the revelations that God, the Great Spirit, has given to humankind through them only exposes our own bigotry, shortsightedness, exclusiveness, and judgmental spirit. Let us appreciate *all* that God has for us. Now it is time for us to begin considering the teachings of each direction: East, South, West, and North.

Part II

◇◇◇◇◇

Teachings of the Four Directions

3

Teachings
of the East

The Direction of Beginnings

When we consider the sundance in the Medicine Wheel it is proper to begin in the East because this is where the sun rises and begins a new day. It is the time of beginning. It is the place of beginning. The color of the East is the yellow or amber color of the rising sun. The Spirit of Innocence, the Spirit of Resurrection, the Spirit of Enlightenment dwell in the East.

Innocence or Justification

Our first teaching of the East comes from this very concept—the time of beginnings. The sun, rising in the East, begins a new day in innocence. We may think to ourselves, "I really blew it yesterday." We may have retired last night feeling guilty for having committed some terrible mistakes during the day, but this is a *New Day*. We all begin this new day in innocence. Some people say that we are making light of sin, but I say, "No! We are making much of grace!" We would much rather place our faith in the grace of the Creator than to spend that spiritual energy entertaining the fear of sin. Remember Job, when he thought about the experience he was going through, and said: "The thing which I greatly feared has come upon me." Fear and faith operate on the same principle—"As your faith is so be it unto you." When Jesus said, "As you sow, so shall you reap," he was appealing to the very same spiritual law. When one sows fear, he or she will reap fear and the fruit of his or her fear. When one sows faith, one will reap faith and the fruit of that faith.

Many people are sick spiritually as well as physically because they carry such a tremendous load of guilt. Everyone else may have forgiven them, but they not only have difficulty in accepting that forgiveness, they are also the last ones to forgive themselves. They find it difficult to believe that they begin a new day with the gift of innocence. Many Christians struggle with this even though Paul the apostle spent so much of his epistle to the Romans expounding on justification by faith. A good definition for the word *justified* is: "Just (as) if I'd (never sinned)." The Native American Indian Medicine Wheel and Paul's teaching in the Bible are saying the same thing—We are innocent, or justified, by our faith in the grace of the Creator. We all need to learn this lesson and shed the cloak of guilt.

Many years ago I heard a black preacher, in the Deep South, declare in his sermon, "God went and done took my sin, and he buried it in the depths of the deepest sea. Then he went and done put a 'no fishin'' sign there." I like that. What a great realization! That is good Medicine Wheel teaching, and it is good apostle Paul preaching. Why would you desire to go fishing for *my* sin? After all, you have no right to talk about my mistakes, but what is more important is that I do not have the right to carry the sense of guilt from them either. If by faith I believe in the Creator's grace, then I can enjoy the blessing of beginning a new day in innocence. I can enjoy a fresh start!

Earlier I quoted Lame Deer as saying that the Medicine Wheel gives us "a trail toward our prayers." A true traditional Indian begins each day by praying to the Great Spirit, God, in each of the four directions. As the scriptures guide Christians in their prayer life, so the teachings of the Medicine Wheel guide Native Americans in their prayers. Ohiyesa, the Santee Dakota physician and author, spoke in 1911 about his people's attitude regarding prayer.

"In the life of the Indian there was only one inevitable duty—the duty of prayer—the daily recognition of the Unseen and Eternal. His daily devotions were more necessary to him than daily food. He wakes at daybreak, puts on his moccasins and steps down to the water's edge. Here he throws handfuls of clear, cold water into his face, or plunges in bodily. After the bath, he stands erect before the advancing dawn, facing the sun as it dances upon the horizon, and offers his unspoken orison. His mate may precede or follow him in his devotions, but never accompanies him. Each soul must meet the morning sun, the new sweet earth and the Great Silence alone!"[1]

The Indian tradition of beginning each day with prayer to the Creator was also practiced by ancient tribal Judaism. "At daybreak you listen for my voice; and at dawn I hold myself in readiness for you, I watch for you" (Psalms 5:3). What kind of prayers may we pray from this teaching? You may turn to the Great Chief of the Above in the East and pray, "Great Spirit, as I begin a new day help me to live this day in purity of mind, body, soul, and conscience." Or our prayer may be one of thanksgiving to the Creator who gives us the assurance that we can start fresh and new. These are good Indian prayers, but they are also good Christian prayers. The ancient Jewish Psalmist was praying this very Indian prayer to the Holy Essence when he prayed, "Create in me a clean heart, O God."

Christians are justified by their faith in Christ. Ancient Jews were justified by their faith in their God (Abraham was counted righteous because he believed in God—Hebrews 11). Native Americans praying the prayer of innocence to the Great Spirit, or Creator God, in the East, are justified by their faith in their God. How many Gods are we talking about? Three or one? They are all the same. There is only one God. He or She is the Great Spirit—Wakan Tanka, the Great Chief of the Above—Hyas Saghalie Tyee, Gitchee Manitou, Theos, Deus, Dios, God!

Resurrection

Another Medicine Wheel teaching of the East is that as the sun rises each morning the Creator is promising us that we can have hope in the resurrection. Last night the sun died, but this morning it arose in newness of life. We also can believe in life after death. There are other ways in which we can believe in resurrection. Many times people speak of something dying within them. They may be speaking of the relationship they have with their mate. They may be speaking about the joy they once experienced in their vocation. Whatever it may be that has died within them, they can pray for and believe in the hope of resurrection. When I officiate at an Indian funeral and pray my prayer to the Creator in each of the four directions, it is to this teaching that I allude as I pray to the Holy One in the East. I pray a prayer of celebration and thanksgiving for our hope in the resurrection. This is a good Indian prayer, but it is also a good Christian prayer. Why is it that many Christians speak of our Native American spirituality as heathen and pagan, while they consider theirs to be the only true way? We are praying to the same God. We are practicing the same spiritual laws. We all pray for the same resurrection. We are all given the same hope of resurrection.

The missionaries told us that our ways were heathen and pagan when they heard us saying that the stone in the middle of the Medicine Wheel was the Great Spirit, or God; when we said that God spoke to us out of the fire in the stones in the sweatlodge. After we became Christians and discovered that John also said that God was like a jasper stone, and that Moses also believed that God spoke to him out of the fire, we knew we were in good company. Were they heathen and pagan like us? Or were we more like them than they could accept?

This teaching about the resurrection provides us with another one of those experiences similar to that which we had with John and Moses. One day, less than a year after we became Christians, the missionary told us that he wanted us to meet with him in a particular meadow up on the hillside before sunrise on the next Sunday. We arrived in the early dawn, and as the sun arose the missionary seemed to become quite excited in his worship. When we asked him, "What are we celebrating?" his answer was *"Resurrection!"* This was an Easter Sunrise Service. Isn't this amazing? When we told him that as the sun arose in the East the Medicine Wheel taught us the lessons about resurrection, he then called us sun worshipers, reminding us once again that we were heathen and pagan. He told us that we must give up these ideas if we expected to become Christians. Now we discovered that the missionary is a sun worshiper just like us. Is he also heathen and pagan like us? He had now joined the company of John and Moses by revealing that he believed exactly what we also professed. We didn't really know what heathen and pagan meant. The missionary's tone of voice, when he said that we were heathen and pagan caused us to believe that we were bad; but when we gained his company in the sun teaching we began to think that maybe being heathen and pagan was good. These missionaries were not too easy to understand, but we know what we believe and we feel good about our relationship with the Creator.

Light Prevailing Over Darkness, or Enlightenment

Now we look at another teaching from the East. Before the sun rises in the morning it may have been so dark that we could not see our hand in front of our face. But as the sun draws closer we experience the dawn, and eventually the glorious sunrise. When the sun has risen we may ask, "Where has the darkness gone?" It has disappeared. The Indian teaching from the Medicine Wheel is that where there is light, there can be no darkness. The darkness cannot apprehend the light. The light swallows up the darkness. Is this also a Christian teaching? Listen to John in his gospel: "The light shines in the darkness, and the darkness has not overcome it," (RSV) John 1:5. What kind of Indian prayers may we pray here? One prayer might be, "Great Spirit, may the light of your wisdom drive away the darkness of my ignorance today." This is a good Indian prayer, but it is also a good Christian prayer. We hear the ancient Jew, David, crying out, "The night shall be light about me" (Psalms 139:11, KJ). God intervened in the midst of David's deep problems and gave him light.

Thus far we have considered lessons regarding beginnings, innocence/justification, resurrection, and light prevailing over darkness.

Other Related Lessons

The lessons about beginnings teach us about birth, rebirth, being born again, renewal, and childhood. When we learn our lessons about light prevailing over darkness we also learn about illumination, guilelessness, truthfulness, the ability to see through complex situations, guidance, leadership, trust, hope, capacity to believe in the unseen, warmth of spirit, love that does not question others, uncritical acceptance of others, watching over others, guiding others, hope for the people, trust in your own vision, ability to focus attention on present-time tasks, seeing situations in perspective, and beautiful speech. The lessons on resurrection brought with them understandings about joy, spontaneity, courage, and the devotion to the service of others. The lessons regarding innocence also taught us about purity, holiness, and vulnerability.[2]

Find the time to receive the sunrise. Feel the power in the hope of resurrection. Enjoy the beautiful cleansing feeling of justification—innocence. Perceive light prevailing over your darkness. Rejoice in enlightenment.

Buffalo or Ox

The buffalo totem is the power of the East in this Medicine Wheel. John and Ezekiel saw it as the ox. The buffalo and the ox are related. They are of the same family. You can cross-breed them and get what is called a "beefalo." In Native American theology we see the buffalo as "The Giver."

Our buffalo brothers and sisters gave of themselves so that we two-leggeds might live. They gave their flesh for our food. They gave their hides that we might have clothing and shelter. Tipis were made from their hides. Every part of the buffalo was used in some way. The buffalo revealed a way of complete giving—complete sacrifice.

The buffalo as the giver is sacrificial, or sacramental. Here we see the Great Chief of the Above revealing power by being sacramental through sacrifice. Sacrament is here

BUFFALO

TREE

understood as being a gift from the deity—God giving God's own self to humankind. We also learn that a person who lives a life of giving to others, even sacrificially, discovers great power. The potlatch, during which an Indian may give away absolutely all of his or her possessions, is ceremonially exercising this teaching. In this way we allow the spirit within us to become sacramental to others through our own lives.

Our Plains Indian brothers and sisters understood this way of life through the buffalo. We experienced this teaching in the Pacific Northwest through the cedar tree. The Creator gave us the cedar tree to teach us this lesson of giving completely. The cedar tree provided our shelter, our longhouses in which we lived, our transportation, our canoes, clothing from the inner bark, baskets for the gathering and cooking of food. The tree sacrificed itself to meet our many needs. It is sacred.

Christians would see this sacrifice in the giving of Christ at Calvary. Christ is the Christians' ox, their buffalo, the one who gives sacrificially, their sacrament. The ox is the burden-bearer, giving of its strength to humankind.

When we learn to give of ourselves to others, we receive illumination; we experience new birth; we feel the fresh winds of new beginnings. We not only need to pray to the Great Spirit in the East each day but we also need to learn how to draw the powers of the East into our own lives. We need to become the living sacrament that God gives to others. I am the buffalo. You are the buffalo.

4

◇◆◇

Teachings
of the South

The sun dances from the East, where it has risen, around to the South, where it reaches its apex at noon. At this time of day one can see the greatest distance. It is the brightest time of the day. The color is white. The Spirit-Who-Sees-Far dwells in the South.

White or the Spirit-Who-Sees-Far

Lessons can be learned from this direction by watching two traditional Native American worshipers at prayer. The two are praying quite different prayers, although both are being guided in their prayer by the same sundance teaching out of the South. One man is a hunter. Turning toward the South he prays, "Great Spirit, help me to see my game at a great distance today." This is applying the teaching to physical need. There is no difference between this prayer and that of a Christian praying that God will help him or her to do well on the job today. They are both concerned with feeding and clothing their families.

The second worshiper at prayer may be the tribe's holy man, or spiritual leader. The prayer may be, "Great Spirit, help me to see into the future. Help me to see those things that will be taking place in order that I may warn or prepare my people for those times." This prayer is prophetic in its nature. The two are very different prayers, yet they are both being guided by the same principle. These are good Indian prayers, but they are also good Christian prayers.

An example of this latter prayer can be seen by looking back at the time shortly before the initial contact between Native Americans and the white man. Indian tribal holy men who were praying this prayer to the Spirit-Who-Sees-Far began receiving a particularly prophetic vision. The Great Spirit revealed to them that the time would soon come when there would not only be red people here, but there would also be yellow, white, and black people coming to these shores. They then recognized this teaching in the Medicine Wheel as they looked at the colors of the four directions: red, yellow, white, and black. The Creator also informed them that unless they cared for these newcomers, the newcomers would die. This prophecy was fulfilled at Plymouth Rock, Jamestown, and many other places. The Europeans would have died if Native Americans had not cared for them. The Medicine Wheel had always taught us about the brotherhood of humans. We had experienced this understanding among our Indian tribes, but now we were being prepared to experience this brotherhood of humankind with new people who were of different color from ourselves.

Green or Growth, Development, Creativity

Some Medicine Wheels have green as the color of the South. This teaching comes from seeing Grandfather Sun climbing higher and higher into the sky as he dances around from the East to the South. The summer sun climbs much higher in the sky than the winter sun. The higher Grandfather Sun climbs into the sky, the more deeply he penetrates Mother Earth. And what happens when Grandfather Sun penetrates Mother Earth? She will become pregnant, she will give birth. As Grandfather Sun climbs higher and penetrates Mother Earth we soon see the green grasses sprouting, flowers budding, fruit trees blossoming—Mother Earth again gives birth! We call it springtime. It is in this sense that the color green is appropriate, as recognized by some tribes. The South now teaches us lessons about being creative and productive, about growth and development. Our prayer to the Creator in the South as a result of these teachings may be, "Creator God, help me to be creative and productive today." We also may pray "Creator God, be born afresh in me today." These are good Indian prayers, but they are good Christian prayers also.

Other Related Lessons

We have learned that the East gives us lessons about childhood. The South teaches us about the growth and development in youth as well as about generosity. This direction, in its extreme warmth, teaches us lessons regarding our passions and emotions, joy and anger. Here we learn about love, compassion, kindness, the heart, loyalty, and gracefulness, sensitivity to the feelings of others. It is here that we learn about goal-setting and determination.[1]

Bear or Man

Once again we look at the powers of the four directions, and here in the South it is the power of the bear. The animals of the other three directions seem to compare very nicely with John's and Ezekiel's visions, but how are we to see the comparison of Ezekiel and John's face of a man with the Medicine Wheel bear of the South? What appears to be a great difference between the visions appears to be a discrepancy only to the Western European mind. The Native American mind can easily understand how bear and man are the same.

The Western mind separates animals from humankind as being of a much lower kingdom, much the same as the Europeans looked upon our ancestors as savages or animals. The Western European Christian has been taught that Adam was given dominion over the animals. A better translation would have taught stewardship. The Christian concept of dominion places humankind over the animals; consequently, people lose their realization of relationship. The Native American mind sees the four-leggeds and the two-leggeds as brothers and sisters. For example, when a four-legged's life is taken in the hunt, prayers are offered thanking the four-legged for sacrificing its life as food for the two-legged brothers and sisters. This is also true for the swimmers and the wingeds. This understanding is also seen in the Lakota Sioux words "Mitakoye Oyasin," which means, "We are all related." Adam had a much closer relationship with the animals than the Western mind can normally comprehend, but the Native American understands it well. The animals were his companions for a long time.

The ancient legends tell of a time when the two-leggeds and the four-leggeds could go back and forth between the kingdoms at will. For example, a four-legged bear could decide to become a two-legged bear, or vice versa. This was in the long-ago time. The Creator finally said we could no longer go back and forth, because we had started arguing with each other. In this long-ago time some of our ancestors elected to remain as four-legged bears, while some of our ancestors elected to be two-legged bears. That is why some of us today are members of the bear clan. We were born into it. Have you ever seen a recently killed bear skinned out? The bear at this time looks very much like a man. This is the Indian understanding of the way it was with Adam and the animals.

In some tribes the bear clan is the warrior clan. In others it is the medicine clan, and in yet others it is the leadership clan. In the bear medicine powers we see the healer, the protector (warrior), and the leader. Here the Great Spirit says that the Holy Essence will be all these things to its family on earth through the bear medicine powers. What is even more important is the fact that as we realize that the Great Spirit dwells in all of us we must accept the responsibility to ourselves and to our fellow humans to allow these powers to flow through us to others. We must become acquainted with the powers of the bear in the South. The lessons we learn here in the Medicine Wheel can also be learned in the Bible. We all need to be protectors. We all need to practice becoming healers. We all can be a leader to at least someone. In our Indian world we respect our elders and look up to them for wisdom and leadership. Even a child is an elder to the younger children and needs to learn how to accept the responsibility of leadership. These powers are for all of us. When we learn all the lessons of the four directions, we can more easily live a balanced life.

We are the human face with the spirit of the bear living in and through us. Thus, an Indian understanding of Ezekiel's and John's visions reveals that we humans are to be sensitive to our responsibilities of allowing the Great Spirit (God) to use his or her medicine powers through us for others in the healing processes provided, whether these be physical, mental, social, or spiritual. We are also to allow these medicine powers to function through us in the protection of others. Is it possible that many of us spend too much time attempting to defend ourselves rather than coming to the defense of others?

Native American people have great potential in leadership, but more of us need to square away our shoulders, lift our heads high, and allow the Great Spirit to work through us in places of leadership. How do you begin? Begin by working diligently with another leader, and it will not be long before you will be leading also. You begin by giving leadership from within the Native American Indian culture. The spirit of the bear is waiting for you to turn to the South for guidance.

5

Teachings
of the West

The sundance in the Medicine Wheel reminds us that the West is the direction of the setting sun, which brings on the darkness of night. The color for this direction is black. There are many lessons that we also learn from this direction. The Spirit of Sees-Within dwells in the West.

Meditation as a Prayer Form

The Spirit of Sees-Within resides in this direction. This is the direction of meditation and introspection. We who are Christians can learn much from the Native American understandings of spirituality at this particular point in the wheel.

In my opinion, the majority of Christians' prayers are those of petition. I sometimes call these the "Oh God, gimme, gimme" prayers. I have the feeling that these prayers far outweigh the prayers of thanksgiving. But what we are talking about, here in the Medicine Wheel West, are not the prayers of petition and thanksgiving, but rather the prayers of meditation. These are the prayers that become true dialogue, where we give the Great Spirit, or God, equal time to dialogue with us. Here, prayer becomes listening rather than vocalizing.

Read the many Native American prayers that have been reduced to writing and you will discover that the prayers of thanksgiving predominate. You will find that this is also true if you attend the sweatlodge and listen to the prayers of our people. Prayers of thanksgiving predominate. Prayers of petition exist, but they are given a place of minor importance. We have also learned the importance of meditation, of listening to God, the Great Spirit, speak to us. This is what happens on the vision quest.

When we pray to the Great Spirit in the East, South, or North, we may pray prayers of thanksgiving or petition. When we turn to the Great Spirit in the West we find that the primary attitude in prayer is to listen.

Imagine that you are a parent with young children at home. Further, I want you to imagine that when the youngest of those children reaches the age of thirty, all of your children are still at home. Yet even further, I want you to use your powers of imagination, and imagine that in all of their years with you they never gave you an opportunity to speak to them. Absurd? Yes! Definitely absurd! Nevertheless, I want you to consider it for a moment. These children may have come to you many times over the years asking for your help. When they were young they may have asked for a dollar for a soda, and when they became a little older they were asking for the keys to the car. These were prayers of petition. Once in a very great while they may have patted you on the back and said, "Mom, or Dad, you are the greatest!" These were prayers of thanksgiving. But every time you wanted to say something to them they replied, "We haven't got time right now, Mom/Dad, we'll see you tomorrow." They never asked for your advice or counsel, and they refused to take time to listen to you when you desired to advise.

This absurd picture is a representation of the way many Christians live. How would you, as a parent, feel if just such an experience should be yours? Hurt? Angry? Bewildered? Despairing? Have you ever considered how the parent of humankind must feel when we have given the same kind of absurd treatment, when we do not take time to listen? Yet, all we experience from our heavenly parent is love—oh, what grace! We need to amend our prayer life. We need to give the Great Spirit, God, equal time. Then we will begin to learn how to pray to the Great Spirit in the West. The next time that you take five or ten minutes to pray prayers of petition or thanksgiving, give the Creator equal time. Take an additional five or ten minutes in silent prayer—listening! Clear your mind so that you can hear.

This attitude of listening is predominant when we go on our vision quests, but it should also become an important part of our daily life.

The Waters of Life

The waters of life come to us from the West. The prevailing rains are from the West. They are life-giving. Without them we could not survive. Grandfather Sun may bring about the birth of new life by penetrating Mother Earth, but that life is not sustained without the nurturing life-giving forces in the waters from the West. We may pray, facing the West, "Creator God, today may your waters of life flow freely through me to others." That is a good Indian prayer, but it is also a good Christian prayer.

The waters from the West are also cleansing and healing. Our prayers for healing are therefore prayed in this direction. The cleansing force teaches lessons in sanctification in the Christian theological terminology. Paul the apostle declares: "But you were washed, you were sanctified" (1 Cor. 6:11, RSV).

Maturing

The sun setting in the West also reminds us of old age beginning to set in. We become more aware of the spirit of the people's past and the knowledge they have gained. Consequently prayers of thanksgiving may be given.

Darkness or Mystery

This direction teaches us the lessons about darkness, about the unknown, about mystery. We learn the lessons of introspection, of going within, meditation, deep inner thoughts, spiritual insight, contemplation, silence, being alone with one's self, thinking or analyzing, and being aware of our spiritual nature.

Other Related Lessons

This direction also teaches us about fasting, sacrifice, perseverance, testing of the will, and humility. Here are the teachings about the fall of the year and adults. In the West we learn about respect: respect for our elders, respect for other peoples' belief systems, respect for the spiritual struggles of others. This direction teaches us about dreams and visions. It is the direction of commitment: commitment to the Creator, commitment to others, commitment to self, commitment to values. This is the direction of participation in ceremonies.[1]

The Eagle

We found that the buffalo is the symbol for the power of the East, and the bear is the power of the South in this Medicine Wheel. The power of the West is the eagle. It is the eagle in all three visions: Ezekiel's vision, John's vision, and the Native American vision. Neither Ezekiel nor John gave us any interpretation or understanding of the meaning of the eagle in his vision; therefore, we turn to the teachings of the Medicine Wheel for a commentary. This, then, is a Native American understanding of those ancient Jewish and Christian visions.

Native Americans recognize that the birds fly freely in the air. They also visualize the spirit world as freely occupying the air. The Bible also speaks of this concept. The birds of the air represent the spirits of the spirit world in Native American spirituality. They are symbolic and therefore are very real. The eagle is the most powerful and most majestic of all the birds of the air. Therefore, it speaks to us as Native Americans of the most powerful and most majestic of the spirits—the Great Spirit (God).

The center of the Medicine Wheel is the sacred altar, because it is the dwelling place of God, the Great Spirit. The outer circle represents the entire universe. This includes the two-leggeds, the four-leggeds, the wingeds, the swimmers, and the crawlers. Our attention is now sharply focused on the fact that we two-leggeds are in the outer wheel and the Great Spirit Eagle, or God, is at the center. But, here in the West, the Eagle or the Great Spirit is also in the outer wheel, in the realm of humans. This then speaks to us of the incarnation of God in humankind. This God becomes flesh. God indwells humankind. The divine is in all of us. Herein is power that is unrealized by many people, both Christian and Native American. It is amazing that so many Christians deny their indwelling divinity when it is so clearly taught in the scriptures. Too often we think of God, the Great Spirit, as being "out there somewhere." These three visions are teaching us that this God indwells. There is divinity within each of us.

The Medicine Wheel also teaches us that the West is the direction for meditation, introspection, looking within one's self. Many people become surprised when they turn to this time of introspection and discover the indwelling presence of the divine. This happens for the first time, in the lives of many people, when they experience their first vision quest.

Thunder and lightning often come from the West, as do the rains. Many Native American traditions see the West as the dwelling place of the Thunder Beings. These are representative of the most powerful in the spirit world. Though they are many, yet they are one. Does this sound like Trinitarian thinking? They are three yet they are one. This is marvelous, for it is God, the Great Spirit, incarnate in each of us that allows for the manifestation of, or display of, the great powers of the Divine Being through us.

We are the Great Spirit's family on this Mother Earth. We are the Great Spirit's sons and daughters. We need to walk in the dignity of our divine family. Let us turn to the West for the cleansing and healing to be found there in meditation and introspection.

As we face the West let us take time to look within ourselves and allow the cleansing and healing spirit waters to flow through us. It is now time to recognize and accept the divine presence of the Eagle within us. The Eagle shall become you, and you shall become the Eagle even as Jesus said, "He that has seen me has seen the Father."

6

◆◇◆

Teachings of the North

The North is the direction from which come the harsh, bitter storms of winter. The color for this direction is red—the color representing life. Our bodies are formed from the red soil of the earth, and blood, which is the life-giving force in our bodies, is red. Red is the color of life. The Spirit of Courage, the Spirit of Wisdom dwells in the North.

Stress or Tension

The winter storms out of the North provide a test for life, and it is the strength and tenacity of life that endures and overcomes the storms. It takes courage and wisdom to be able to face and weather the storms. It is a rare individual who actually enjoys being out in a storm and being buffeted by it. But none of us escapes the storms of life: in the home, on the job, in the marketplace. We do not enjoy these storms. We do not like storms, but our Indian teachings out of the North say that storms are good for us, because they are a path to growth. How many times have you stepped outside, after a stormy night, and said,

"Breathe in that fresh air. Didn't last night's storm really clear the air?"

We learn many of our lessons from the storms of life. How often we have said, "I sure learned a lesson from that one!" There may be easier ways to learn our lessons of life. However, some lessons are learned only from the storms of life. That is why the Creator does not allow a single one of us to escape them.

By enduring and overcoming the storms we are strengthened for greater tests in life. We can learn a lesson from the trees. A tree that grows in a sheltered valley is protected from the severity of the wind. Growing next to the river it grows quickly and has large, soft rings. The lumber that is cut from this tree is soft and good only for such things as sheathing, to be covered over. However, the tree that grows on a high mountain ridge faces tremendous windstorms and draws little moisture from the soil. The small amount of moisture causes the tree to have small, tight rings. Surviving the many years of buffeting by the winds, from the time it is a small tree until it has reached maturity, creates a toughness. It is this tree that will give us our strong bridge timbers. So it is with life. Many, if not most, of our greatest leaders grew up in a storm-filled life. In surviving they give to us the strength of leadership and wisdom.

As we turn to the Great Spirit, or God, in the North for our time of morning prayers, we may pray: "Great Spirit, I give you thanks for the lessons you taught me in yesterday's conflict." Or, "Creator God, I give you thanks for giving me strength and wisdom as I face the confrontations of life." You might also pray a prayer of petition: "Grandfather, give me the strength and courage that I will need for today." These are good Indian prayers. They are also good Christian prayers.

The history of ancient tribal Judaism, as reflected in the

Old Testament, gives us many stories of personal as well as collective group conflicts. We learn these same Native American Indian teachings as we study these ancient tribal people. David the Psalmist alluded to these teachings in his morning prayers when he said, "The night shall be made light about me" (Psalms 139:11, KJ).

Paul the Apostle addresses this teaching for Christians when he speaks of the Great Spirit as God and says, "God is faithful, and he will not let you be tempted beyond your strength, but with the temptation will also provide the way of escape, that you may be able to endure it" (1 Cor. 10:13, RSV).

Other Related Lessons

What are some of the other lessons we learn from the North? The North also speaks to us of completion or fulfillment. All of the cycles are completed here in the North. This is the direction of the completion of the life cycle; therefore, the teachings about old age, the elders, eschatoalogical lessons, the end times, the ability to finish what we begin, realizing how everything fits together. Out of these teachings come instruction and guidance on how to live a balanced life: lessons about wisdom, insights, moderation, justice, understanding, speculation, discrimination, prediction, interpretation, imagination, integration of all intellectual capacities, capacity to dwell in the center of things, to see and take the middle way. From the lessons about storms we learn valuable lessons about freedom, freedom from fear, freedom from hate, freedom from love, freedom from knowledge, about detachment and problem solving. Our intuition is made conscious: calculating, organizing, categorizing, and criticizing.[1]

This is the direction in which all things come together, giving us our traditions and ceremonies for which we are thankful. They remind us to learn from and respect the traditions and learnings of the elders.

Cougar or Lion

The animal totem for the North in this Medicine Wheel is the cougar. In Ezekiel's and John's visions it is the lion. The cougar is our North American mountain lion.

This is the final totem of the four directions and tells us something about the power of the North. It is the fourth of the revelations of the attributes of the great Spirit, or God. This is the fourth of the aspects of the powers of the universe, or of the powers of the Great Spirit—God.

What do we see as the spiritual understandings of John's and Ezekiel's visions when we use the Native American Medicine Wheel as a commentary on each of them?

The cougar is the best climber of all the members of the cat family. It climbs the highest. This reminds us that the Great Spirit desires to manifest this power in each of our lives by helping us to climb to the highest points of the potential in our personal lives. This lesson is also taught to us by the eagle, who soars the highest of all the wingeds. This suggests to us that the Great Spirit is the Great-Chief-of-the-Above, or the God of the heavens. Two-leggeds who respect the indwelling presence of the Great Spirit and allow the deity within to manifest the power of the Sacred Mystery through them will find that they may soar high, or climb high, philosophically and spiritually.

The cougar also enjoys roaming the earth. We are reminded of the old cliché, "Some people are so heavenly minded that they are of no earthly good." But this cougar spirit of Grandfather dwelling in us is not only the God of the heavens, but is quite earthy—the God also of the earth. We learn much about God, the Great Spirit, from Mother

Earth. There is a good balance between the spiritual highs and the earthiness of this God, and therefore a good sense of balance is experienced by people who seek to understand this Sacred Mystery who dwells within each of us. This spirit helps us to remain well grounded and balanced as we roam and search for truths and meaning in life.

The cougar is also a hunter. This reminds me of Jesus speaking of himself as a "fisher of men." He was a hunter. The spirit of the cougar helps us as hunters in our search for spiritual, philosophical, and sociological truths in life. Here we see the feminine nature of God—the Goddess. The female cougar is a better hunter than the male. Those of us who are biologically male need to be more aware of the feminine side of our nature when we are in this hunt. Much of modern Western Christianity has lost this understanding of the feminine nature of God and of ourselves. Native Americans pray not only to Grandfather but also to Grandmother (God/Goddess). The ancient tribes of Israel understood this. They regarded God as speaking of herself as a mother. God says, "As one whom his mother comforts, so I will comfort you" (Isaiah 66:13, RSV). God also speaks of herself as "a woman in travail" (Isaiah 42:14, RSV). The Christian New Testament speaks of our being "born" of God. Does this God have a womb? Is this not a picture of the feminine nature of God? When we gain as clear an understanding of the feminine nature of God as we now have of the masculine nature of God, then maybe we will be able to walk a more balanced life. We will then be able to allow this God to manifest himself or herself through us in a more realistic way.

Let us face the stress and tensions of the North with faith in the Creator's power to give us courage and strength for life's tests.

Part III

Circles

7

Cycle Teachings of
the Four Directions

The Circle

The circle is one of the most powerful symbols in Native American spirituality. It speaks to us of the eternal nature of life. You can find neither the point of beginning nor the point of ending to the circle. This teaches us that life is unending. We can have a hope in eternal life. These lessons of life come to us from the Medicine Wheel, the Native American's Bible. The Medicine Wheel is known to many of our people as the Wheel of Life. We see life as being beyond the concept of "time consciousness." It is outside of time, cycling forever and forever. Are not these teachings also Christian teachings? Consider, "Beloved, we are God's children now; it does not yet appear what we shall be, but we know that when he appears we shall be like him, for we shall see him as he is" (I John 3:2, RSV). Or, "For this corruptible must put on incorruption, and this mortal must put on immortality" (I Corinthians 15:53, KJ).

The circle also teaches us of life in its vertical nature, the fullness of life in the present. The sweatlodge is circular, and as we enter it we are reminded that it is the symbol of the entire universe, the center of which is the presence of the Great Spirit. The sweatlodge is another Medicine

Wheel, and it teaches us that we can experience and enjoy the fullness of life at all times.

The powerful sundance is also experienced in a circle. The sundancers dance in a circle about the central flowering tree that is the sacred altar. Outside of the circle of dancers is a circle of prayer sticks in the colors of the four directions. The dancers are enclosed and protected by a circle of people in an attitude of prayer. Outside of this circle is a circular path that supporters of the dancers dance upon as well as the sundancers themselves before they enter the sacred circle about the altar. Outside of this last circle is yet another circle. This one is the arbor where the community of family and friends are much more than spectators. Their spirits are at one with those of the dancers. There is a very close bond between each and all in this community. Those in the outermost circle are also in supportive prayer for the dancers. When I stand in the arbor I feel that I am in a circle about Calvary where Jesus, the greatest sundancer of all time, was pierced and affixed to the central flowering tree. I sense that I am on sacred ground (see Figure 8).

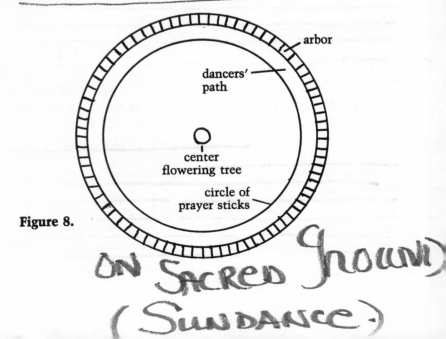

Figure 8.

arbor

dancers' path

center flowering tree

circle of prayer sticks

ON SACRED Ground

(SUNDANCE.)

Traditionally, we also experience the circle when we sit down in an Indian council. These councils were never held sitting in straight rows, white man's style, but in the powerful circle. In many churches Christian people sit in straight rows with a singular view of the altar; they all see the altar from the same perspective. This translates into theological concepts with exclusivist views. Everybody must see things as we do or else they must be wrong! This produces a narrow-minded, bigoted, judgmental type of spirituality. Therefore, many Christians are constantly arguing and debating with other Christians for their own singular view. Proselytization is common, for Christians are certain that they must convert everyone to their own view. On the other hand, you never see one tribe attempting to convert another tribe to its own tribal view; and it is important to note that all tribes do not observe the same rituals and concepts within their spirituality. This thought of attempting to convert or proselytize among tribal spiritualities is absurd to Native Americans, because we sit in the circle with the altar at its center, and every one of us has a different view. But we recognize that all of these views are valid, and our own spiritual journeys are empowered as we listen to the views of others in the circle.

When our people on the plains were taken out of their tipis and placed in the government rectangular houses, on the reservations, we stopped fighting the white man in an attempt to defend ourselves. We had lost the circle, the source of our power, and therefore had no spirit left within us to defend life.

Black Elk says, "There is much power in the circle, as I have often said; the birds know this for they fly in a circle, and build their homes in the form of a circle; this the coyotes know also, for they live in round holes in the ground."[1]

The circle, among the Shawnee, celebrates the fullness of what the finisher Kigimanitou has done, according to our Shawnee friend Neeake. The great house for the celebration is set as a large circle around a center pole. Other poles are set at a specified distance from the center pole to form a circle. Upon each pole is a skin, a feather, a carved object, or a plant to represent the whole of creation. This power revealed in the finisher's care of creation surrounds the one who enters the circle. It is a microcosm of all life to remind the celebrant that such power always surrounds us in the journey through life, on the circle from birth to death and rebirth on a new plane of existence. Our present circle is the womb of life nurturing us until we can be born into a higher and fuller oneness with the finisher. These ideas are very prominent for many in the sweatlodge and in the sundance ceremony.

My Tlingit friend Jack Strong tells of the first day he went to school. He entered through a square door into a square room and sat at a square desk. The windows were square. The blackboard was square. The books on his desk were square, and when he graduated they put a square cap on his head and gave him a square diploma. They then expected him to know how to put square pegs in round holes!

The circle can be seen everywhere we look. Both the sun and the moon are round, and they travel in circular orbits. Everything in nature is round. The circle teaches the way for a full and balanced life.

We speak of the family circle, circles within circles. First, there is the immediate family circle, and then the extended family circle including grandparents, aunts, uncles, and cousins; then the tribal circle, as well as the circles of each of the world's nationalities. All of humanity is in the outer circle.

The ancient tribal people of Israel also recognized the power of the circle. Ezekiel spoke of wheels within wheels. The Israelites found great power within the circle in the circumambulation of the walls of Jericho. Job speaks of "God walking in the circuit of heaven." Were these ancient people sun worshipers? Or was the sun a powerful symbol of God for the ancients as it is for many Native Americans? Did these ancient Jews see God in the sun as it made its circuit through their skies? Isaiah spoke of God when he said, "It is he who sits above the circle of the earth" (Isaiah 40:22, RSV). Was he recognizing the Great Spirit's power as Creator? In their hymnal, the Psalms, the Jews sang of "God's circuit unto the ends of the heaven."

John, in the New Testament, tells us of his vision of elders in a circle about the throne of God. This certainly reminds us of an Indian council. There is also the story, in the New Testament, of the apostle Paul being stoned and his body being dragged out of the city as if he were dead. His followers and friends made a circle about him and prayed for him, and he revived, arose, and departed with them.

We need to encircle one another with our love and care. There is great power in surrounding others with our support. Alone we may be weak, but we feel strength from others when they surround us with their love and care. This speaks to us of our need to gather ourselves together as a means to encircle others who are in need, with our love, support, and prayers. Today, many call this networking.

Pottery reflected the Medicine Wheel five thousand years before Christ in the Near East.

Already in the pottery styles of the middle fifth millennium B.C., for example, balanced geometrical organizations of a circular field make their appearance, with a binding figure in the center symbolizing the integrating principle: a rosette, a cross, or a swastika. In late symbolic compositions this central position was occupied by the figure of a god, and in the earliest city-states the same divinity was incarnate in the king; in Egypt, in the pharaoh.[2]

Every circle has its four directions that create cycles of many kinds: the life cycle, the annual cycle, and many other cycles. We now take the teachings of the four directions and cycle them in the circle, thus revealing lessons of a more compound nature. We should keep in mind one thing as we study these various cycles. We need to keep all four directions in balance with each other in each of the cycles. Our wheel will be out of balance if we concentrate too much on one direction while neglecting the others; likewise, our life will be out of balance.

Four Faces, or The Life Cycle

Recall that in the Sundance Medicine Wheel we see the sun rising in the East, beginning a new day. This is the direction of beginnings. This is the place of beginnings in the life cycle—the direction of childhood and its teachings. The sun in the South gives us growth and development; this the direction of youth and their teachings. The West is the direction of adults. The North, which is the culmination and completion of the cycle, is the direction of the elders.

The East—Childhood
Do you still have the Medicine Wheel stones on your floor? In my Medicine Wheel the stones in the East are

yellow or amber, the stones in the South are white, the stones in the West are black, and the stones in the North are red. Use your imagination and imagine that your stones are the colors of the four directions. Now reach down and pick up one of the white stones of the South and replace it with one of your amber stones of the East. Doesn't it look out of place? This is the child who has become a youth, but is still very childish. This child may have grown and developed physically, but there has been a lack of leadership and training in his or her social and spiritual understandings. What is very sad is when you must replace a black stone with the amber stone, indicating that the individual has become an adult but is still very childish. Many parents fail in providing spiritual leadership and training for their children, because they do not believe it is that important. They raise their children to believe that life owes them a living, not so much by intentional teaching but by their own actions. They do not provide proper and adequate cultural training for their children. Then they wonder why their children are still quite childish when they become adults. What happened that they didn't grow up?

There is a great difference between being childish and being childlike. Jesus said, "A little child shall lead them." Many of us have forgotten the child that we were, or the child that is buried within us. The child is in awe of his or her world. Matthew Fox would tell us that the mysticism that we need so desperately in our Western culture lies in the child within us. Remember that the Medicine Wheel teaches us that the East is the direction of resurrection. The child within us can be resurrected.

Let us consider another problem as we look at the faces of all four directions. The child who is facing the center is also facing whom? The child is facing the adults, but in today's modern American culture there is a large percentage of double-income families. Mom and Dad have both put in a long day at work and now they are trying to get caught up on their household duties. One of their children comes to them with a question, and their answer is, "Can't you see that we are very busy right now. Go outside and play. We'll talk to you later." But, later does not come. They are too busy to listen to their children. The children are facing the center of the wheel and therefore are facing the adults, but the parents have their backs turned to them. They are facing away from the wheel. By the time the children have become youths they no longer ask their parents any questions. They are now in the South, the direction of growth and development, but their backs are now turned away from the wheel of life. They are now facing away from the wheel. The grandparents in the North may be still facing the center of the wheel, but the youth do not hear them. They have turned away. Consequently, no one is paying any attention to anyone else. It is sad to say that this is the picture of life in too many American homes today. We Native Americans, who have become acculturated into the dominant culture, have fallen into this same trap. It is time for us to learn once again from the Medicine Wheel and initiate changes in our homes. All of us in the family need to turn and face the center. In doing so we will not only be facing each other, but together we will be facing the sacred altar. There will be a greater sense of wholeness in our families.

The South—Youth

This is the direction of growth and development. This is also the direction of creativity.

We may have learned our childhood lessons well, but we certainly do not want to miss the great catalysts of life that can be discovered in our youth. These can make the difference between happiness or misery in our adult life. Parents cannot opt out of their responsibilities just because their children have outgrown childhood and have become youths. Parents are needed as much as ever. Too many parents seem to have the attitude that their children have now grown up and should be given their independence. They now feel free from their parental roles of responsibility in the development and growth of their children. Although these youths do need a much greater sense of independence, the parental role becomes one of even greater importance. Parents need to help provide the catalysts to the childhood teachings that now cause the "lights to come on," providing new insights, new understandings about the world that these children are experiencing.

This is also the time to develop creativity. Young people have great potential in creative abilities. Every opportunity that is possible should be provided them, especially at this stage of their lives. This can provide a very fruitful adult life for them.

The West—Adults

The West is the direction of introspection. We have now become adults, and it is time to look within ourselves and attempt to discover who we really are. Most of us think that we know ourselves quite well. At times we wish that other people understood us as we understand ourselves.

The truth is that we are cognizant of only a certain portion of the large area of our lives. Others know things about us of which we are not personally aware. This is an area of our lives that is very real, although unknown to us. Then there is an area of our lives that is unknown to both ourselves and to others. At times it takes a special incident to cause us to become aware of something about ourselves that was hidden in this unknown area of our lives. It is here that the vision quest becomes so very important to us, as we dwell in the West of our life cycle. Many times we discover very important things about ourselves in these experiences.

We entertain our greatest responsibilities in the life cycle while we are here in the West as adults. But the Thunder Beings are here to empower us. In our Christian theology we would say that God's spirit empowers us.

The North—Elders

We highly honor and respect our elders. They have lived through all four directions of the life cycle. They have gained wisdom through their life experiences.

At many non-Indian church potluck dinners, parents of the baby-boomer generation often demand that the children be served first. This will never happen at an Indian potluck dinner. The elders are always honored by being served first. Children need to learn to honor their elders by example. The elders hold within themselves the power of hope for the younger generations. There is a great loss to any culture when this is ignored.

Each of us is an elder to someone. The ten-year-old is an elder to the eight-year-old. This brings us to another important lesson from the Medicine Wheel. We are in trouble if we are concerned with the teachings of only the direction we are now dwelling in. For example, we are in trouble if as adults we are interested only in the adult teachings of the West. It is very important for us to continue to understand and caress the child within us. We also need to continue to recognize the youth within us and work intentionally in the area of growth and development. We desperately need to continue to be creative. Matthew Fox says that "A study done a few years ago in America found that 80 percent of six-year-olds but only 10 percent of forty-year-olds were creative. Thus between six and forty, creativity is killed in our culture."[3] America is in trouble! We also need to recognize the elder within us. In other words, no matter where we are in the life cycle, we need to recognize how the teachings of each of the four directions apply to us at the present time.

Thus far we have been talking about our own individual lives in relationship to the teachings of the four stages of life: childhood, youth, maturity, and culmination. We need to be aware that every nation, culture, or organized group of any kind also travels through this life cycle.

Where is the United States, as a nation of people, in this cycle? Was the colonial era our childhood? Did the Declaration of Independence usher us into our youth? Did we evolve into our stage of maturity at the time of the industrial revolution? Are we already facing the end of a cultural era as we have known it? On the other hand, I am reminded of the time that someone reportedly asked Mahatma Gandhi what he thought of the American culture, and his answer was, "I think it is a good idea, they need one." Maybe we are still in the infancy of our childhood, and yet need to grow up. We are somewhere in the life cycle as a nation, but just exactly where are we?

Where is Christianity in the life cycle? Was the period of the apostles, and the spread of Christianity throughout the period of the ten imperial persecutions, the childhood of the religion? Was the Romanizing of Christianity its youth? Did the Protestant Reformation usher in its period of maturity? Has the current ecumenical movement brought Christianity to its elder stage—its final stage as it has been known? If so, what is next for Christianity?

There is another lesson to learn from the Medicine

Wheel. We mentioned earlier the fact that the circle teaches us the lessons of eternal life. Life goes on! We discover the teachings of death and rebirth when we couple that teaching with this one of the four stages of life. Every year we experience Thanksgiving and Christmas, and then watch the old year die and see the new year being born. We continue to travel around and around this circle year after year. We plant a kernel of corn in the ground and watch it die only to be born again and spring up into a new life.

Is Christianity approaching such a time? There is much that is practiced in Christianity that needs to die and find a rebirth. The fundamentalist mentality needs to die and find a more creative rebirth. The Fall/Redemption theology has developed into an anthropocentric breed of Christianity. It places those who follow it in a spiritual prison. Fall/Redemption Theology needs to die. It needs a rebirth into a Creation Theology. This would not be anything new, but rather would allow Creation Theology simply to come full circle around its own Medicine Wheel to where it was at the beginning of the present cycle in early primitive Christianity.

I predict that this will take place by the end of the twenty-first century. I also predict that there will be a merging together of the Medicine Wheels of the other great religions of the world. Christianity will still be Christianity, but it will become very different from that we experience today. It will joyfully incorporate the teachings of the other great religions of the world into its own understanding or worldview. It will go through a death and rebirth. It must travel through the cycle of its own Medicine Wheel. Christianity will become more powerful! It will then fulfill the hunger of many who are desperately seeking more than Christianity now gives them. All seekers will then be able to participate in the great Medicine Wheel!

Four Seasons, or the Annual Cycle

Again, the East is the direction of beginnings. Therefore, it reminds us of spring in the annual cycle. The South is the place of warmth and talks to us about summer. The sun sets in the West, and the day begins to come to its maturity and close, bringing us to the fall. The North brings on the cold winds of winter—the fulfillment and culmination of the cycle.

The Four Races

East/Yellow; South/White; West/Black; North/Red
Some of our Native American brothers and sisters believe that it is not right for some of us Native Americans to share the ancient teachings and traditions with non-Indian people. We need to ask ourselves, "Which is the most powerful, the Medicine Wheel or me?" The answer is, "The Medicine Wheel, of course!" After all, how can I protect something that is more powerful than I am? The Creator did not give us the Medicine Wheel so that we might need to protect it. The Medicine Wheel was given to save us! Many believe that the Medicine Wheel is very ancient, so ancient, in fact, that at one time it belonged to all people. It belonged to the earliest humans, but most of the races of humankind either lost or abandoned it for other cultural mores.

We need to listen to the Medicine Wheel as it talks to us. We look at the colors of the four directions, and it teaches us that one quarter of the Medicine Wheel belongs

to the red race, and one quarter belongs to the yellow race;
one quarter belongs to the white race, and one quarter
belongs to the black race. We are all related. This concept
is expressed in a very beautiful way by the Lakota Sioux
people when they say "Mitakoye Oyasin," which means,
"All my relations," or "We are all related." This goes far
beyond just seeing that all races of humankind are related,
but recognizes that we two-leggeds are also related to the
four-leggeds, the wingeds, the swimmers, the crawlers, and
every living thing that grows upon the Earth Mother.
There is the commonality we all share; from the dust of
the earth we were formed, and to the dust of the earth we
shall all return. We are all related. We are all one.

The Four Basic Elements of Nature

There are four basic elements of nature: air, fire, water,
and earth.
Daylight breaks and we can see our world about us, as
we could not do when it was yet dark. The East is the
direction of *air*. The South is the direction of warmth, and
is the direction of *fire*. Our rains come from the West, and
this is the direction of *water*. The North is the direction
of *earth*.

Four Things That Breathe

The East, the direction of air, is the direction of the
wingeds who fly in the air. The four-leggeds were created
before the two-leggeds, and their direction is the South.
The West is the direction of the two-leggeds, and the North
is the direction of those that crawl—the crawlers.

Four Things Above the Earth

The East is the direction of the *stars*. The South in its warmth is the direction of the *sun*. The West is the direction of the *moon*, and the North is the direction of the *planets*.

Four Parts to Green Things

The East is the direction of *roots* to all green things; when we journey back to our own roots we are turning to the East—the place of our beginnings. The warmth of the summer South causes the plant to burst from the ground giving us the *stem*, and so we see growth and development. The West brings us to the time of maturity, and gives the plant her *leaves*. The North, the culmination of the cycle, brings us to a time of ripening in age and thus provides the plant with its *fruit*.

Four Divisions of Time

The East is the time of *day*—the sun rises in the East and brings us daylight—and the West is the time of *night*. The South is the direction of our moon cycles, *months*. The North, the culmination of all cycles, is the direction of that time known as the *year*.

Animals of the Four Directions

In this Medicine Wheel the cougar, buffalo, bear, and eagle are the medicine totems of the four directions. We saw in Chapter 1 how these four animals in the Indian vision compared with the "four beasts" in Ezekiel's and John's visions. In Chapters 3 through 6 we studied each of these individually, at the close of each chapter on the four directions. There we considered what the teachings are regarding each animal.

Now we need to ponder how these animal totems relate to each other for the fullness of the powers, and how the teachings might be applied for the living of a balanced life. We have seen that the buffalo is "the giver," the symbol of complete sacrifice. The bear is the warrior, the medicine power bringing healing (physically, socially, mentally, and spiritually), the leader. The eagle is the Great Spirit incarnate within us, in recognition of our own divinity. The cougar is our high climber philosophically and theologically, while also remaining very earthy. The female cougar is the hunter; therefore, the cougar is the Goddess nature that indwells us.

Some of our television evangelists have become great hunters (cougar). They gather and gather, building great empires. But they have not given equal time and energy to develop the buffalo within themselves—the givers. They appear to be living lives that are out of balance.

Our government has worked diligently to develop a worldwide image of the warrior—bear. It also makes a pretense at being a healer sociologically, but denies any responsibility for spiritual leadership out of the fear of mixing church with state. The pendulum does not find a good center of balance but intentionally swings far to one side, and we wonder why we have such tremendous problems with drugs and violence. Our government's Medicine Wheel is out of balance. Our government could become more concerned with spiritual values without becoming sectarian. Some spiritual values are held in common among all religions, such as the common belief in a divine being, a Creator, a power higher than humankind.

Tom Brown, Jr., has said,

Animals, like humans, make in life the mistakes that will ultimately lead to their death, either physically or on a spiritual and emotional level. . . . People and animals that stay on the same paths in life will eventually wear themselves into ruts—a complacency to life born of the false security, comfort, and monotony of that path. Soon the ruts become so deep that they can no longer see over the sides. They see neither danger nor beauty, only the path before them, nor do they abandon that path so often traveled, for fear of losing their security and entering the land of the unknown.[4]

We need to keep a sense of balance by equally walking the paths of the powers of all four of the directions.

All of us desire to walk well-balanced lives, but very few do so. We tend to overdevelop certain areas at the sacrifice of others. We consider some aspects of our lives more important than others, but the truth is that they are all equally important. We need to give equal time and attention to all four of the powers as they flow through us, which will bring us to a greater sense of balance. This will take place in direct proportion to the success we have in allowing all four of these powers to develop within us in a balanced manner.

The Four Gospels

Is the Medicine Wheel able to relate to the non-Indian world? Let us examine a few examples. If the Medicine Wheel relates to truth wherever it may be found, then we should be able to look for those truths in other cultures.

People have asked me whether or not the four Gospels

may be seen in the teachings of the Medicine Wheel, and
if so, how?

The East, or John

We begin with the East, the direction in which the sun
rises. The darkness of the night flees from the advancing
sun. The teaching is that the darkness cannot overcome
the light, but the light always overcomes the darkness.
Therefore, as Indian people, we may pray to the Great
Spirit in the East that the light of wisdom might dispel
the darkness of our ignorance.

This is the teaching of the Gospel according to John 1:4,
5. John says that the greatest medicine man who ever
lived, Jesus, was the light of the world. He also said that
where there was light there could be no darkness. Wisdom
is a theme in this Gospel. The Gospel of John is in the East.

The South, or Matthew

The sun reaches its zenith in the South. This is the time
of day that one can see the greatest distance. Our prayers
may focus on the need to see great distances. This is true
in all ways: physically, spiritually, socially, and philosophically. A person may pray to be able to foresee events
that are to take place in the future (seeing prophetically).
Only one of the four gospel writers refers back to the ancient prophecies of the Jewish tribal prophets. This was
Matthew, who consistently refers back to the prophecies
of Isaiah, Jeremiah, and others. Matthew's concentration
was on the South, upon those who were looking into the
future.

The West, or Luke

Luke, who was a Greek doctor, was educated in the Helle-
nistic teachings of the Greek philosophers. The Greeks

were constantly looking for the perfect human: physically, socially, mentally, and spiritually. Luke presented Jesus as the perfect divine man. Luke began early in his Gospel to lay the foundation for his exposition. In Chapter 2, verse 52, he spoke of the child Jesus as increasing in wisdom (mentally), and stature (physically), and in favor with God (spiritually) and man (socially). Luke's emphasis was on perfection and cultural idealism.

The West is the direction of introspection, meditation, contemplation, clear self-knowledge, and commitment to the path of personal development. This is the direction of healing, of being drawn closer to perfection. Luke is the Gospel of the direction of the West.

The North, or Mark

The North is the direction from which come the storms. This is true not only geophysically but also in the realm of our individual and collective lives. We need to cultivate our powers of endurance for these storms. In this direction we become people of courage and action.

Mark is the shortest of the four Gospels. One might call it the paperback version of the Gospel, written to the Romans, who did not have time to read long books or to philosophize as did the Greeks. The Romans were busy militarily conquering the world of their day. The majority of the men were soldiers who were either conquering or posted at the outstations of the empire maintaining its protection. These were people of action and conquest. Mark presents Jesus as a man of action and conquest. This is the Gospel that contains the bulk of the miracle stories. This is the direction of the North.

The four Gospels are in the Medicine Wheel. The Medicine Wheel Gospels present the full story of Jesus through

representation in all four directions. The Medicine Wheel sees Jesus portrayed as wisdom and enlightenment that overcomes the darkness of our world; the fulfillment of the words of the prophets; the guide that leads us to perfection; the overcomer and conqueror of all evil.

John Wesley's Quadrilateral

Let us try another example of how well the Medicine Wheel can apply itself to the teachings of the non-Indian world. Is it possible that truth, wherever it may be found, fits into the teachings of the Medicine Wheel?

John Wesley, the founder of Methodism, believed that all of our doctrines should be able to stand the test of 1) the Scriptures, 2) Experience, 3) Reason, and 4) Tradition. This has become known as the "Quadrilateral."

It is through this window that Methodists perceive their worldview. Is this also a Native American way of perceiving the world? Is there any similarity between the two? Let us explore and see.

East or the Scriptures

The Medicine Wheel is the window through which many Native American people view the world. As we turn to the East, the Medicine Wheel teaches us that this is the direction in which the sun rises, dispelling the darkness of the night. We understand from this that the light of knowledge and of wisdom dispels the darkness of our ignorance. Ancient tribal Judaism says, "Thy word is a lamp unto my feet, and a light unto my path" (Psalms 119:105, emphasis mine). Methodist Indian people would then see this direction of the Medicine Wheel as relating to the scriptures in the quadrilateral.

South or Experience

The South is the direction of growth, development, and creativity in the Medicine Wheel and may be seen as experience in the quadrilateral.

West or Reason

The West is the direction of meditation, introspection, contemplation, and insight. This then becomes the direction of reason in the quadrilateral.

North or Tradition

Finally the North is the culmination of all the directions in the Medicine Wheel. It is the direction of fulfillment or completion. When we look at the cycle of the seasons of the year the East is spring, the South is summer, and the West is fall. We see the North as the completion of the cycle with winter. When we see the cycle of life, the East is childhood, the South is youth, the West is adulthood, and once again the North is the culmination of the cycle, this time with the elders. So it is with all cycles in the Medicine Wheel: the north is the culmination, the completion, the fulfillment of the cycle. Likewise, the combination of the teachings of scripture, experience, and reason gives us the culmination of the cycle in our traditions. Tradition belongs to the North.

But the traditions of Western Christianity have formed out of the experiences, reasoning, and scriptural understandings of Western or European peoples. The question that is being raised here is, "What will Christianity feel, taste, and smell like if these same scriptures develop into a tradition through the experiences and reasoning from

Native American concepts and values derived from the Medicine Wheel? What will be the resulting worldview?"

It is important for us as Native Americans to consider these questions. Non-Indian people as well as Christian Native Americans who consider these questions could become the force for a new birth within the Christian church. This could produce a revitalization that is much needed and overdue in the Western world.

Interfacing Wheels

What happens when we create a complete Medicine Wheel in each of the four directions? We will have four Medicine Wheels interlocked or interfaced within a larger Medicine Wheel (see Figure 9).

How do we read this model? What does a Medicine Wheel interpretation or understanding of the quadrilateral tell us?

The East of the East is readily seen as scripture's impact upon scripture. R. A. Torrey once said, "There is no other commentary on the Bible so helpful as the Bible itself."[5]

The South of the East is experience's interpretation of scripture. Each of us brings our own cultural experiences to the scriptures, and we interpret the scriptures in the light of those experiences.

The West of the East is reason's understanding of scripture. This is the direction of Systematic Theology as well as the various philosophies of religion. Those who reason from an understanding of the Oriental philosophies will discover that the scriptures reflect insights very different from those received by Western philosophical perceptions. The same is true when we look at the scriptures through the windows of Nature and the Eastern philosophies of

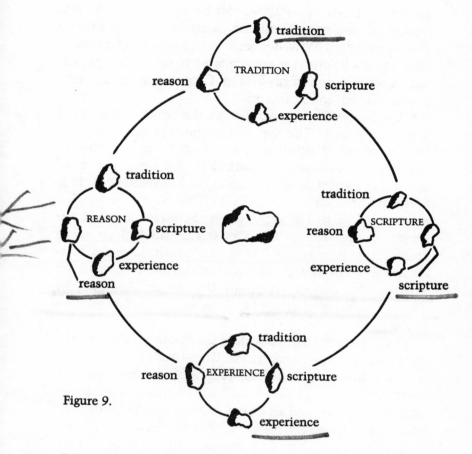

Figure 9.

life. A circular spirituality anticipates that we will search for truth through all of the windows available.

The North of the East is tradition's interpretation of scripture. But which of the traditions shall we follow? Shall we follow the Catholic or the Protestant tradition? If we choose the Protestant, then which of the current Protestant traditions? Or should we decide to follow a medieval or primitive Christian tradition? We can also raise an array of questions if we decide to follow a Native American tradition. There are many of these traditions! They are legion! Why not look at the scriptures through all of the traditions that are available to us? This approach can be very rich and rewarding. It can enhance and empower our current worldview.

What happens when we turn to the South of the main Medicine Wheel? The East of the South is the scripture's interpretation of experience. This is diametrically the opposite perception we entertained in the East, where we interpreted scripture from our cultural experiences. It is here, in the South, that we allow the scripture to give understanding to our experiences. Fundamentalist, Conservative, and Evangelical Christians can feel far more comfortable here in the East of the South. Liberal Christians will feel more comfortable in the South of the East. Why not be eclectic and enjoy the perceptions of both? That is circular spirituality. That is living the fullness of life.

When we turn to the South of the South we find experience's impact upon experience. These are the people who do not follow any particular philosophy of life or creed. They simply live and let live. They live from one experience to the next, and all of life is understood through the windows of these experiences. This can be a valuable direction in which to stand if we use it in conjunction with all of the other directions. But, we are in trouble if this is the only direction in which we stand. We then become like a ship without a rudder, drifting aimlessly on the high seas of life at the mercy of every wind and current. The balanced life comes from experiencing the entire circle.

The West of the South is reason's understanding of experience. This is the direction of the many divergent schools of psychology that provide us with good windows through which we may see and understand life. But they do not give us a complete understanding of life. We need the entire circle.

The North of the South is tradition's interpretation of experience. Again, each tradition will give us a different interpretation.

Now we turn to the West. The East of the West is scripture's interpretation of reason. This may be what Isaiah had in mind when he wrote, "Come now, let us reason together, says the Lord" (Isaiah 1:18, RSV). Was Paul the apostle in this direction when Festus with a loud voice said to him, "Paul, you are mad; your great learning is turning you mad" (Acts 26:24, RSV).

The South of the West is the direction of life's experiences giving expression to reason. It is here that people attempt to understand the philosophies of life through the lens of their own life experiences. This is similar to the South of the East where we bring our cultural experiences to bear upon scripture for an understanding of life.

The West of the West is reason's impact upon reason. This is the direction where the various philosophies of life come to bear upon each other. It is also here that the various schools of systematic theology come to bear upon each other.

The North of the West is tradition's interpretation of reason. This is where the many religious traditions of the world attempt to give understanding to the world's philosophies.

The North is the direction of tradition. The East of the North is the scriptures' impact upon tradition. The Catholic tradition and each of the Protestant traditions differ accordingly as to how they have allowed their understanding of the scriptures to formulate their tradition.

The South of the North is experience's impact upon tradition. Christianity is quite different throughout the world as traditions are formed out of the very different experiences of cultural expression.

The West of the North is reason's impact upon tradition. Here we see how various traditions have formed as a result of the influence of the local philosophies of life, such as a Christian philosophy or a Buddhist philosophy.

The North of the North is tradition's impact upon tradition. This is never allowed by the fundamentalists of the different religions of the world, and rarely allowed among the liberals. This is, no doubt, the weakest point in this particular study of the Medicine Wheel. This is the main focus of this book: to bring differing traditional belief systems to bear upon each other and to allow a process of eclectical healing to begin, thus providing us with the greatest ecumenical environment that humans have ever experienced. This is the weak link in the chain. This is where we must concentrate our efforts.

We have just concluded a brief experiment of placing each of the four cardinal points of John Wesley's quadrilateral in each of the four directions and allowing them to reflect off of each other in the Medicine Wheel. As a result there have been some very interesting revelations. You may use this model with any cycle teaching of four. Place each cycle in each of the four directions and then allow it to speak to you.

How about individual teachings that have not been presented to you in a cycle with four views? Let us take the concept of "Wisdom" as an example. Begin by writing a definition of wisdom from the teachings of each of the four directions. Then look for a key word from each of the four directions in your definition. Now take these four words and cycle them in each of the four directions of your Medicine Wheel. The end result will be that you will receive sixteen fresh insights in your growing understanding of wisdom. You may do this with any lesson or concept. Try it! It will provide you with a richly rewarding experience!

Matthew Fox's Four Paths

Matthew Fox is a Dominican scholar, a leading proponent of Creation theology, which is the very base of Native American spirituality. It is fascinating to see how his "Four Paths," as revealed in his book *Original Blessing*, compare with the Sundance teachings in the Native American Medicine Wheel.

East or Path One: The Via Positiva
Matthew Fox titles "Path One, Befriending Creation: The Via Positiva (the way of the positive)." Fox says,

> Western civilization has preferred love of death to love of life to the very extent that its religious traditions have preferred redemption to creation, sin to ecstasy, and individual introspection to cosmic awareness and appreciation. Religion has failed people in the west as often as it has been silent about pleasure or about the cosmic creation, about the ongoing power of the flowing energy of the creator, about original blessing.[6]

He continues by saying that this path is a way of "affirmation, thanksgiving, ecstasy."[7] Fox deals with ten themes related to this path: "1) The creative energy of God; 2) Creation as blessing and the recovery of the art of savoring pleasure; 3) Humility as earthiness; 4) Harmony, beauty, justice as cosmic energies; 5) Trust; 6) Panentheism; 7) Our royal personhood; 8) Realized eschatology: a new sense of time; 9) Holiness as cosmic hospitality; 10) A theology of creation and incarnation."[8]

Fox calls us "back to human relationships to earth, air, fire, water."[9] He declares that "The healing process of making whole and integrating also includes a return to one's origins . . . to examine anew our pre-existence, both in the historical unfolding of the cosmos and in the Creator's heart."[10]

His teachings about this path are the teachings of the East in the Medicine Wheel—the place of our beginnings, our origin; the place from which light comes.

West, or Path Two: The Via Negativa

Fox's Path Two is the opposite direction—"Befriending darkness, letting go and letting be: The via negativa." This is the West in the Medicine Wheel. He speaks of this as the place of meditations as is also taught in Native American theology from the teachings of the West. He decries that his church (the Catholic Church) has replaced meditations with mortifications.

He speaks of the mystical tradition being lost in Protestantism which has resulted in "an exaggerated fall/redemption preoccupation with sin, so that one's sinfulness became the proper object of meditation."[11] He speaks of letting go and letting be.

Fox's teachings about this path are very much the teachings of the Native American understandings of the teachings from the West in the sundance in the Medicine Wheel.

South, or Path Three: The Via Creativa

Fox's "Path Three: Befriending creativity, befriending our divinity: The via creativa," is directly related to the teachings of the South in the Medicine Wheel. This is the direction of growth and development. This is where we can come to understand our relationship with the Creator, our divinity.

We recall that Fox reveals how "A study done a few years ago in America found that 80 percent of six-year-olds but only 10 percent of forty-year-olds were creative. Thus between six and forty creativity is killed in our culture; this means, theologically speaking, that God is killed. God is aborted in a culture where imagination and juicy creativity are not celebrated. This way we invite violence."[12] Christianity needs to be Indianized! Let us reconsider the teachings of the scriptures from the teachings of the South in the Medicine Wheel, and from the pre-Augustinian days of the ancient church.

North, or Path Four: The Via Transformativa

Fox's Path Four is that of the via transformativa (the way of transformation). This is "Befriending new creation: compassion, celebration, erotic justice."

The North in the Medicine Wheel is the culmination or the fulfillment of the cycle. Fox's Path Four is the culmination and fulfillment of his teachings of the other three paths.

Fox sees the traumatic problems of Western civilization as being a direct result of Augustinian fall/redemption and original sin teachings. He recommends a return to creation theology and original blessing teachings, which are so in accord with ancient Judaism and early pre-Augustinian Christianity.

These teachings are very much alive in Native American theology. Maybe Native Americans need to become missionaries to the modern Western Christian Church, calling it back to its pre-Augustinian roots and to a neo-creation theological understanding of our God-given relationships. Thus we will be more appropriately prepared for the biases as well as the benefits of our current cultural existence.

The Famous Four Horsemen of The Apocalypse

We might consider another point of interest while we are on the topic—the colors of these four directions. In Chapter 1 when we looked at the Medicine Wheel vision as compared to the visions of Ezekiel and John, we considered only the fourth chapter of the Book of Revelation. The following chapter in the Book of Revelation tells us about a book with seven seals, and Chapter 6 discusses the opening of those seals:

> Now I saw when the Lamb opened one of the seven seals, and I heard one of the four living creatures say, as with a voice of thunder, "Come!" And I saw, and behold, a white horse, and its rider had a bow; and a crown was given to him, and he went out conquering and to conquer. When he opened the second seal, I heard the second living creature say, "Come!" And out came another horse, bright red; its rider was permitted to take peace from the earth, so that men should slay one another; and he was given a great sword. When he opened the third seal, I heard the third living creature say, "Come!" And I saw, and behold, a black horse, and its rider had a balance in his hand; and I heard what seemed to be a voice in the midst of the four living creatures saying, "A quart of wheat for a denarius, and three quarts of barley for a denarius; but do not harm oil and wine!" When he opened the fourth seal, I heard the voice of the fourth living creature say, "Come!" And I saw, and behold, a pale horse, and its rider's name was Death, and Hades followed him; and they were

given power over a fourth of the earth, to kill with sword and with famine and with pestilence and by wild beasts of the earth. (Rev. 6:1–8, RSV)

The opening of the first four seals reveals the famous Four Horsemen, and what are their colors? Red, pale, white and black—the colors of the four directions. And who revealed them? The four living creatures or powers of the four directions revealed them! Absolutely amazing!

Four Main Human Philosophies

Amber Wolfe, a psychotherapist in private practice who has lived in the Far East, speaks of the four basic human philosophies and relates them to the Medicine Wheel with: 1) The Oriental mindfulness philosophies, dealing with the mind and thinking, in the East; 2) The Western linear philosophies, dealing with the body and physical sensation, in the South; 3) The Eastern spiritual philosophies, dealing with the spirit and intuition, in the West; and 4) The Nature (aboriginal) philosophies, dealing with the heart and feelings, in the North.[13]

Four Areas of Life

There are four areas to every human life, no less, no more. Everything that takes place in an individual's life is found to be in one or more of these four areas. They are: 1) the physical area of life, 2) the mental area of life, 3) the sociological area of life, and 4) the spiritual area of life.

Each of us has been given a physical body. It is impossible to exist without it. Each of us has been given a mental aptitude, and we spend much of our lives developing this area. We are social creatures by nature, and every human being has a spiritual nature.

To deny any of these areas is to commit suicide. Absolute denial of the physical is biological suicide. A person is committed to a mental institution when he or she commits absolute denial of the mental area of his or her life, thus committing mental suicide. The hermit has denied the social area of his life, thus committing social suicide. Many people do not realize that in denying the cultivation and development of their spiritual lives, they are in the process of committing spiritual suicide, and the Medicine Wheel of their lives is out of balance.

In order to live a balanced life we must give equal care and attention to these four areas: the physical, mental, social, and spiritual. This is our Medicine Wheel teaching. The East is the direction of the mental area of life, the area of enlightenment and knowledge. The South is the direction of the physical area of life, the area of growth and development. The West is the direction of the spiritual area of life, the direction of the vision quest and introspection. The North is the direction of the social area of life, the area in which we find the stress and tensions of interrelationships that are so important and necessary to life. Once again it is important to state that these are the prime directions for each of the four areas. It is important to understand the teachings of each of the four directions and how they relate to each other.

Luke recognized the importance of these four areas when he wrote his Gospel presenting Jesus to the Greeks as the perfect, divine human being. He says, "And Jesus increased in wisdom (mentally) and in stature (physically), and in favor with God (spiritually) and man (socially)" (Luke 2:52, RSV; parentheses mine).

Cycling of the Individual Teachings of the Four Directions

In Chapters 3 through 6 we dealt with the teachings of each of the four directions. What happens when we look at these individual directional teachings in a collective manner in all four of the directions?

Let us consider the teachings about *wisdom* as an example. Some Medicine Wheels consider the North as the prime direction of wisdom because we learn the wise ways of life as we struggle with life's tensions, and as we also learn wisdom from the elders. Other Medicine Wheels see the East as the prime direction of wisdom because it is the direction of enlightenment. The truth is that wisdom, and all of the other Medicine Wheel teachings, are learned from all four of the directions. We cannot write a full definition of wisdom until we have written it with understandings from all four directions.

Enlightenment comes from the East to give us knowledge. Thus we gain knowledge about wisdom. We soon learn that knowledge and wisdom go together. Some people gain knowledge but do not use it wisely. Wisdom is knowledge in action in a wise manner. In turning to the South we come to understand wisdom more perfectly as it grows and develops within us. It is here that wisdom also gives us greater vision. In turning to the West we continue to write our definition of wisdom by adding concepts about wisdom regarding the inner self, cleansing, healing, and the powers of the universe. In turning to the North we learn the wisdom of the elders, achieved by traveling the many annual cycles and experiences of life. We never learn any of the lessons of the four directions completely if we only study them from their one prime direction. All of the lessons of life must be studied as they reflect off of each of the four directions of the Medicine Wheel. This will give us good balance in our lives.

The Four Philosophies of India

Joseph Campbell, the well-known mythologist, tells us that

The philosophies of India have been classified by the native teachers in four categories, according to the ends of life that they serve, i.e., the four aims for which men strive in this world. The first is DHARMA, "duty, virtue," of which I have just spoken, and which, as we have seen, is defined for each by his place in the social order. The second and third are of nature and are the aims to which all living things are naturally impelled: success or achievement, self-aggrandizement, which is called in Sanskrit ARTHA; and sensual delight or pleasure, known as KAMA. These latter two correspond to the aims of what Freud has called the id. They are expressions of the primary biological motives of the psyche, the simple "I want" of one's animal nature; whereas the principle of DHARMA, impressed on each by his society, corresponds to what Freud has called superego, the cultural "thou shalt!" In the Indian society one's pleasures and successes are to be aimed for and achieved under the ceiling (so to say) of one's DHARMA: "thou shalt!" supervising "I want!" And when mid-life has been attained, with all the duties of life fulfilled, one departs (if a male) to the forest, to some hermitage, to wipe out through yoga every last trace of "I want" and, with that, every echo also of "thou shalt!" Whereupon the fourth goal, the fourth and final end of life, will have been attained, which is known as MOKSHA, absolute "release" or "freedom."[14]

Interesting! These four philosophies are the four directions in the East Indian Medicine Wheel, and they can be aligned with the concepts and teachings in our Native American Medicine Wheel. The ARTHA is in the East, where the rising sun dispels our darkness bringing enlightenment and self-aggrandizement. The KAMA is in the South, the direction of sensual delight or pleasure. The DHARMA is in the West, where duty and virtue become important when we turn to our time of introspection and "looking within." The MOKSHA, the culmination of the cycle, or its fulfillment in an individual's life, is attained by going out into the forest, "to some hermitage, to wipe out through yoga every last trace of 'I want!' and, with that, every echo of 'Thou shalt!'" This is our Native American vision quest in which our Tamanawas comes to us as our guiding spirit to lead us through life. This is what Paul the apostle is speaking of when he talks about "walking not after the flesh, but after the spirit." This is also why Paul would likewise say, "It is not I that liveth, but Christ who liveth in me (Gal. 2:20)." These three different ways of saying the same spiritual truth are surely powerful medicine!

TEACHINGS

DHARMA   EAST
ARTHA   South.
KAMA   West
MOKSHA   NORTH .

(SAMES)

INDIA   NATIVES

8

The Inner Circle of Seven Stones

The center stone, at the intersection of the four directions, reminds us of the Great Spirit, Grandfather, Creator God. The seven stones in the immediate circle around this sacred altar are symbolic of the seven spirit messengers of the Great Spirit.

John's vision, as recorded in Revelation, speaks of these as seven torches, seven lamps, or the seven eyes of God, according to which version you may be reading; but all of these versions interpret these as "the seven spirits of God" (Rev. 4:5l, KJ).

In Revelation chapter 1, John speaks of the seven golden candlesticks, which he then identifies as being symbolic of the seven churches. Revelation chapters 2 and 3 contain letters to those seven churches. Each of these seven letters is directed to the spirit messenger of that church. Most versions use the word *angel*, but this word is a transliteration, and not a translation. The word is *messenger* when it is translated. Thus we have seven spirit messengers.

Paul the apostle said that the spirit of God searches all things and reveals them unto us. That is good Native American theology. The spirit messengers give us visions of revelations from the Great Spirit.

The stones in this inner circle (see Figure 10), as well as

7 SPIRITS OF GOD = 7 MESSENGER

owl

cougar

raven

hawk

sacred altar

coyote

bear

Figure 10.

wolf

those in the outer circle, are symbolized by four-leggeds and wingeds. These will vary from tribe to tribe in the various Medicine Wheels, but they reveal special messages of identification to those who follow the traditional ways.

The scriptures reveal them with such terminology as "Spirit of Wisdom," "Spirit of Understanding," "Spirit of Power," "Spirit of Might," and so on. Native American theology identifies the same understandings with the teachings that come from the symbols of the four-leggeds and the wingeds.

As we allow our Native spirituality and our Christian faith to integrate with each other, we allow ourselves to enjoy new insights for our journey on this pathway of life.

The seven spirit messengers of the seven stones in the inner circle of our Native American Sundance Medicine Wheel around the sacred altar are the owl, the cougar, the hawk, the coyote, the wolf, the bear and the raven.

The Owl

The owl is the bird of the shadows, the darkness, the night. It is the messenger of death. An example of this Indian teaching is seen in the book, *I Heard the Owl Call My Name*.[1] This is a story about a young priest who was sent to minister in a small Canadian Indian village on the Pacific Northwest coast. The bishop knew what the young priest did not know—that the priest had less than two years to live. He was faced with the death and funeral of a young child upon his arrival in the village. He heard the mother of the child say that she had heard the owl call the child's name. The priest did not know what that meant, and it was explained to him that she consequently knew that her son was going to die. The story ends with the priest telling an old matriarch of the tribe that he had heard the owl call his name. His own death took place shortly thereafter.

Bearwalk[2] is another book that talks about this Indian teaching. The book begins with the story of an old medicine man who died and was buried by the church, facing the East, the direction of resurrection. He had made a request of his young friend, Richard, to dig up the grave, after he was buried, and turn him so that he would be facing the West. "The old man always used to say that burying an Indian facing East is like walking into the future backwards."[3] Richard was being faithful to the old man's request:

> The moon was higher now, its bluish tinge brighter, resisting the night. The branch of a nearby tree quivered in the moonlight, capturing Richard's attention. He spotted the silhouette of a small Snowy owl. How bloody appropriate, Richard thought, his eyes filling with tears. . . . A branch on which the Snowy owl

perched quivered and shook as the bird took off, flying straight over Richard's head. . . . Richard shivered. "What kind of answer is that old man? I just kept my promise to you. Now don't you honestly think I deserve better than that?" Richard thought about the owl—the symbol of Death. "That owl has been plaguing me all of my life . . . ." It was Richard's sixth summer that the owl—and death—first touched his life. . . . It was a happy life, filled with laughter and love. On the day it all changed, Richard was playing with his cousin Louis. Richard and Louis were not the best of friends by any means; there was something about Louis's manner that set him apart. His dark, knowing eyes seemed to pierce the souls of children and adults alike making them uncomfortable in his presence.

The two boys were lying side-by-side that day under the leafy shade of a maple tree, watching the June clouds drift by when it happened. Richard's eyes were half-closed, dreaming, and he barely noticed the shadow of the bird circling overhead. It was Louis who sat up and calmly announced: "Your father is dead."

Richard turned to him incredulously, his mouth open, speechless.

"There's been an accident. He has drowned. Go home now and see if what I say is not true."

"You're lying, Louis. You're lying!" Richard cried as he jumped up and began to run, his legs pumping to the cadence of the words Louis had spoken. Your father is dead. Your father is dead. But when he burst into the house and searched his mother's face, he knew Louis had spoken the truth.[4]

These two stories highlight a teaching found in the belief systems of many Indian people of different tribes. The owl is the messenger of death. These Indians, on reading the story of Moses and Pharoah in the Old Testament, would see the death angel of the last plague as the spirit of the owl.

Another side to this teaching about the owl is the owl does its hunting in the night. It can see better at night than any other of the wingeds. The ability of the owl to see so well in the darkness of the night speaks to us of the spirit of the owl, as a spirit messenger, guiding us through the darkness of our night of bereavement. Therefore, the owl not only gives the message of impending death, but when it continues to manifest itself over a period of time to someone, it may be giving the message to that person that he or she is being called to a ministry to the bereaved. There are both the negative and the positive sides to this teaching. The owl becomes symbolic of the Great Spirit's Spirit messenger announcing death, but it is also teaching us that the Great Spirit ministers to us at the time of death in our bereavement. As Christian Indians we then see this as one of the seven understandings of the office and work of the Holy Spirit, the third person of the Trinity. The Holy Spirit is seen here as the comforter, the Paraclete.

We have often heard people speak of "the wise old owl." It is here that we recognize the spirit of wisdom at work among the spirit messengers. Christian Indians would see this as one of the gifts of the Holy Spirit, "A word of wisdom."

The Cougar

We studied the cougar in the latter part of Chapter 6 as the animal totem of the North, one of the animal totems of the four directions. We recognize the importance of the cougar both climbing high and also being at home on the earth when we apply these teachings to this spirit messenger of the Great Spirit. This spirit messenger is both heavenly and earthly. The Great Spirit sends us this spirit messenger to help us find a sense of balance in our daily walk, our spiritual journey. This is the God-given spirit of conscience.

The cougar is also a great hunter, and it is the female cougar that is the best hunter. Have you ever noticed that the churches have far more women in them than men? These hunters are in their search for truth. Jesus said, "Follow me and I will make you fishers of men." He was talking to fishermen. He probably would have used the term "hunters" if he had been talking to hunters. This concept belongs to the spirit of the cougar. We who are biologically male need to turn to our feminine nature to guide us in our search for theological or philosophical truth. In considering the office and work of the Holy Spirit, the third person of the Trinity, the cougar as a spirit messenger of the Great Spirit is the one who "searcheth all things, yea, the deep things of God, and reveals them unto us" (1 Corinthians 2:10, KJ).

The Hawk

Hawks soar high and are in close communication with the Great Spirit. Some tribes refer to them as small eagles and use their feathers in sacred ceremonies.

This spirit messenger brings gifts of deliberation and foresight to the two-leggeds. Here is the spirit of prophecy. Those who prophesy are allowing this spirit messenger to speak through them.

Hawks are particularly fond of rattlesnake meat. Two-leggeds who are in close touch with this spirit messenger are not afraid to attack the "rattlesnakes" of this world. They become fearless with the power of this spirit messenger. There are many examples of this fearlessness in the histories of Native American people, ancient Jews (David and Goliath), and Christians.

The Coyote

The coyote is the changer. This is also seen in the coyote's mineral totem—petrified wood. Petrified wood is wood that has changed over time from wood to stone. The legends about the coyote are numerous, and many of them have to do with coyote changing something from one thing into another, or changing himself or herself into something else. He or she is not only a creator but also a great teacher, a trickster teacher.

This spirit messenger brings to us not only the creative nature of the Great Spirit but a teaching nature as well. Christians would see this attribute of God in the Holy Spirit as the teacher. This is where we find inspiration and new creative ideas or concepts.

The Wolf

The wolf is the pathfinder and protector. The wolf as the spirit messenger of the Great Spirit leads us and guides us in the way we should go. This is our spirit guide who not only comes to us on our vision quests and gives us a sense of direction for our lives but also continues to guide us on the path all of our lives. The Christian New Testament speaks of this as "receiving a call from the Lord," or of the state of "being called." Would it not be better to blaze a trail for others to follow than to create a rut by walking in someone else's trail?

The idea of God being our protector is readily seen all through both the Old Testament and the New Testament.

Native Americans see it in their Bible, the Medicine Wheel, in the wolf, as the Great Spirit's messenger to us.

There is a great sense of family in the wolf pack. This spirit messenger is continuously reminding us that we are members of the Great Spirit's family. This is the spirit messenger who keeps us sensitive and aware of our "Mitakoye oyasin," the fact that we are all related, as we discussed earlier.

The Bear

In some tribes the bear clan is the medicine clan, whereas in others it is the warrior clan. The bear clan is always a leadership clan. This concept of bear medicine translates into the bear as spirit messenger of the Great Spirit in revealing God as our healer, and the one who will fight our battles for us.

How many times do we read stories in the Old Testament of how God fought Israel's battles for her. In the New Testament, in Ephesians 6:11, we read that we are to "put on the whole armor of God" (RSV), and that we are to endure hardness as a good soldier of Jesus Christ. These scriptures would have us believe that we are to allow the Holy Spirit, the active agent of the Godhead, to manifest God's self through us as both warrior and physician. This is the work of the Great Spirit through the spirit messenger bear for Native American people.

The Raven

Some tribes speak of the raven as "the wisest of all the birds, and the first one to know all about the land." Other tribes know the raven as the spokesperson for the Great

Spirit. Two-leggeds through whom the spirit messenger raven manifests himself or herself are the spokespersons of the Great Spirit to this world: ministers, priests and priestesses, the shaman, medicine men and women, holy men and holy women, the spiritual leaders.

It is interesting to note that not only do Native Americans see the raven as the first to know all about the land, but when we read the stories of those ancient tribal Israelites, we find their story about Noah, and again it was the raven who first knew all about the land. Why do some people think that their culture is correct and all others are wrong? Why can we not accept the fact that we do not all see our world alike, and that each person's worldview is valid for him or her? There is an interesting story about Elijah in the writings of these ancient tribal Israelites. He was out in the wilderness complaining to the Great Spirit that he was the only one left who was serving the deity. This God told him that there were many others who were faithful to the old ways. The point of interest in this story is that it was a raven who brought food on a daily basis to Elijah. The spirit messenger, the raven, was active in this ancient Bible story.

These seven spirit messengers of the Great Spirit are seven reflections or understandings of the Spirit of God in Old Testament Judaism and the Holy Spirit or the third person of the Trinity in Christianity.

The number seven is a very important number in Old Testament tribal Judaism. It is a number of perfection, completion, fulfillment. The God of the Jews created the heavens and the earth in six days and rested on the seventh, completing and fulfilling the perfect work of creation. Samson had seven locks to his hair giving him perfect and complete strength. Solomon's House of Wisdom had seven pillars indicating that it was a place of complete and perfect wisdom. Seven is also a special number for people of other spiritualities.

The Seven Chakras

Recently, at one of our talking circles, I was presenting the teaching of these seven spirit messengers. Spirit Woman (Evelyn Jenkins) was present and she responded, "Why those are the seven chakras." She went on to explain:

Owl—The First Chakra

The first chakra is the root chakra. It is found at the base of the spine, and its color is red. The symbol is a circle divided into four quadrants that is often recognized as a flaming cross (see Figure 11).

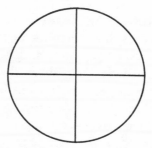

Figure 11.

This is the Creator's pure energy connecting with the human body to give life force and to bring divine animation to physical form. When this chakra is in balance the life force moves smoothly. Fear, the shadow self or the subconscious ego self, throws this chakra out of balance. Like the message of the owl regarding death, the root chakra must function or it too will announce death of the organism. The root chakra and the owl both are messengers of death under certain circumstances. Any message of death also speaks to us of life. Root chakra and the owl are both about life and the Creator's gift of love as well as about death and the ego's gift of fear.

Cougar—The Second Chakra
The second chakra is called the spleen chakra. Its color is orange, and the symbol is a wheel divided into six segments (see Figure 12).

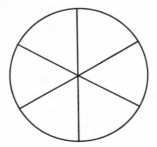

Figure 12

Like the cougar the second chakra relates to balance. The cosmic or Creator's life force is drawn into the body through the first or root chakra and it rises like sap in a tree into the second chakra, where the one pure force is divided into two being experienced in human life through harmony and balance. The two major expressions of the life force are (1) Sexuality—creating or replicating human form, and (2) Creativity—bringing form into manifestation from desire and idea. These two forces require balance and are also thought of as the feminine (sexual) force in the universe, and the masculine (creative) force in the universe. Before the Creator's pure energy can act upon creation it must move into the two forces. Harmony and balance in the second chakra allows this force to act, create and transform to the next higher plane.

Hawk—The Third Chakra
The third chakra is called the naval or the solar plexus chakra. It's color is yellow, orange, or red (like the red-

tailed hawk). The symbol is a wheel with ten equal segments (see Figure 13).

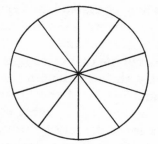

Figure 13.

This chakra, like the hawk, communicates fearlessness, personal power, and courage to the organism and to the outer world. This chakra is also a center of prophecy since it aligns itself with the "gut" in the human body and reminds us of the hawk's exceptional vision powers. Much of human safety and knowingness comes from a "gut" feeling. This chakra is all about knowing the future through body awareness. It is called "the mind within the body."

Coyote—The Fourth Chakra
The fourth chakra is called the heart chakra. Its color is green or golden light. The symbol is a wheel divided into twelve equal parts (see Figure 14).

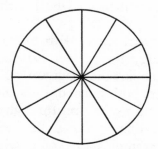

Figure 14.

The heart chakra is the fulcrum point of the seven chakras. The door from the physical experiences to direct communication with the spirit realm is through the opened heart chakra. The coyote is the changer and a creator! So are we changed, even when we resist. Life's experiences open our heart. Actually, the coyote is the Medicine Wheel messenger that opens the heart chakra.

The experiences of life that crack open our ego-protected hearts are exactly the experiences needed to change us from shadows and masks of the illusion to wide-awake messengers and actors of the higher consciouness of the divine. Humans learn the most through heartbreak, betrayal, the trick or con—through loss of what the ego perception thought was most important. The truly opened heart chakra brings a person to true humility and surrender. Only then can the spirit be heard within or acknowledged without.

It is through the opened heart chakra that we become inspired to acts of divine creation. Without love through humility the ability to be awed by the creation would not exist. Human beings create beauty around them when the heart is divinely inspired.

Wolf—The Fifth Chakra
The fifth chakra is called the throat chakra. The color is silvery blue like the color of the moon (the wolf howls at the moon). The symbol is a wheel with sixteen segments (see Figure 15).

The throat chakra deals with humans using the Creator's pure energy for perfect expression of the truth. When the third chakra (hawk-power) and the fourth chakra (coyote-heart) are both opened, then the Creator's energy is clear for perfect expression through the throat chakra. It comes as soul sounds through the spoken word, in song, toning, chants, tremelos, or even howling.

As the wolf, the pathfinder, leads us in the way that

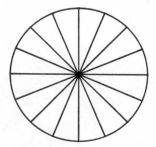

Figure 15.

spirit wants us to go, we can move with spirit when we express the truth of our purified being. We cannot express truth of spirit unless we know it within, unless we can hear the soul's call. The pathfinder wolf is our spiritual guide or leader totem. In human affairs those who guide in the highest way are those who have clear expression from a purified heart of pure intention. These human leaders direct us in the way we should go. If we are to "be called" by the Creator we must hear it first within ourselves through purification. Then we can express it as a call to others. Those who continue to blaze new trails, like the wolf pathfinders, must first be guided by the call from within, the divine expression from the Great Spirit.

To express the truth we must also become the pathfinders for those who prefer the illusion. Is it not so that the true expressions of those who have changed human consciousness such as Christ, Martin Luther King, and Gandhi, defended the truth with their lives? They are, as the wolf, the protectors of the truthful pathway even unto the death.

Bear—The Sixth Chakra
The sixth chakra is called the brow chakra, or the third eye. The color is blue indigo or blue-black (black bear).

The symbol is a circle in two halves divided into ninety-six segments (see Figure 16).

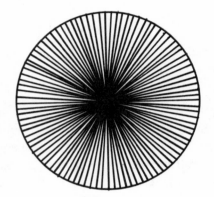

Figure 16.

The sixth chakra, or third eye, allows one into two doors simultaneously. The first door is to access the knowing of other worlds through visions—the dreamtime space. It is here that we are to learn from these visions what is required to heal the organism or system, whether that may be the human body or the Earth Mother's body—the whole world.

Edgar Cayce, a devout spiritual healer, accessed all of his healing information by entering a trancelike state and "seeing" what spirit would reveal to him. Many scientists have had sudden "insights" that verify their theories, which thus become factual. The third eye is open through meditation and contemplation like the bear. Humans must allow the quieting of the chattering mind in order to open to spiritual power. Go with the cave-hibernating bear and open to the void. One whose sixth chakra is opened is one who has access to all knowledge.

Through the second door of the third eye one learns how to use the vision's gifts of spirit to do battle with the darkness, with ignorance, or with the shadow self. All true healers or medicine people are also warriors. They know, as did Christ, that ignorance is the greatest disease. Perceptions must change in order for healing to take place. The old must be destroyed. Those with open third eyes know too much to remain ignorant. They cannot remain passive observers of life, but rather become the great warriors and healers of change.

Raven—The Seventh Chakra
The seventh chakra is called the crown chakra. The color is violet and golden-white light. The symbol is a wheel with twelve inner segments (see Figure 17).

Figure 17.

The seventh chakra opens the way for us to commune directly with God or the Great Spirit. We now see God face to face. This is the most direct connection in union with the Creator. The visions of power accessed through the sixth chakra guide human beings to fully surrender to the divine, thus experiencing "enlightenment," that is, being filled with or being one with the light. This is a literal experience. All truly holy men and women, the saints, are like the Christ—depicted with halos or the enlightened crown of their heads.

These enlightened humans, like the raven, become the direct messengers of God or the Great Spirit. They are the ones who know the desires or the true will of the Great Spirit. They are the revelators to humanity. They know the way home like the raven knows all about the land. The enlightened ones bring spirit to earth and earth to spirit.

Evelyn Jenkins credits her understanding of the chakras to *The Chakras—A Monograph* by C. W. Leadbeater.

S'iva, Vishnu, Brahma

This is a Trinity. Christians may substitute "the Father, the Son, and the Holy Ghost" if they wish. Out of these come seven powers for man; Ernest Wood calls these *The Seven Rays*.[5] The teachings of the Seven Rays have been influenced by the Buddhist and brahminical teachings.

1. *The man of will, seeking freedom through mastery of self and environment: the ruler.*

We gain mastery of self as we look within ourselves through meditation and introspection. Thus we may learn to discipline ourselves gaining mastery of self. This teaching is found in the West of the Sundance Medicine Wheel. We gain the understandings of our environment from each of the four directions. From the West we learn the environmental lessons regarding the waters, i.e., the rains, rivers, lakes, and the sea.

This is the spirit messenger known as raven in the inner circle of seven stones, the direct messenger from the Great Spirit to humankind and the first to know all about the land.

2. *The man of love, seeking unity through sympathy: the philanthropist.*

This is the teaching of the South in the Sundance Medicine Wheel where we learn our lessons regarding our passions and emotions, joy and anger, love, compassion, kindness, the heart, loyalty, gracefulness, sensitivity to the feelings of others. This is also the direction where we can see the greatest distances: physically, spiritually, sociologically, philosophically, thus helping us in our quest for unity.

This is the bear in the inner circle of seven stones, which is the most human of the seven, and from whom come many of the Medicine societies.

3. *The man of thought, seeking comprehension through the study of life: the philosopher.*

This, again, is learned from the teachings in the West of the Sundance Medicine Wheel, where we take time for vision questing, meditation, looking at life.

This is the trickster teacher the coyote in the inner circle of seven stones.

4. *The man of imagination, seeking harmony in a threefold way: the magician, actor, and symbolical artist or poet.*

This is the direction of the South, the direction of creativity.

The Sundance Medicine Wheel teaching from the inner circle of seven stones reveals that this is the hawk who can display in the heavens with magical flights, a real actor. The hawk's flights flow in an artistic and poetic manner.

5. *The man of thought, seeking truth in the world: the scientist.*

This is the direction of the East where we find enlightenment and knowledge, and the wolf, in the inner circle of seven stones, the pathfinder and protector.

6. *The man of love, seeking God as goodness in the world: the devotee.*

This is the South as seen in number two in the Sundance

Medicine Wheel, and the bear as in number two of the inner circle of seven stones.

7. *The man of will, seeking the beauty that is God in the world: the artist and craftsman.*

This is the South as seen in number four. The inner circle of seven stones reveals that this is the cougar whose medicine color is blue/green—blue for the Great Spirit (God) in the sky, and green for the earth (world), its customary habitat. The cougar, in this teaching, moves around to the South and climbs high to the Creator, thus bringing the Creator's creative and esthetic powers to our earth world as great medicine power for artists and craftspersons.

The Sundance Medicine Wheel teaching would see this Eastern Medicine Wheel as being the seven stones in the inner wheel, which are the seven spirit messengers with their messages, or powers, for humanity in the outer wheel. This Eastern Medicine Wheel ignores the teachings of the owl in our Native American Medicine wheel, and the teachings of the North are not considered when we attempt to understand those seven rays through the teachings of the four directions. This Eastern Medicine Wheel ignores the dynamics of receiving messages from the Great Spirit (God) through life's tensions.

Ancient Mesopotamia

Joseph Campbell tells us that during the rise of Mesopotamia, ca. 3500 B.C., "The center of fascination and model for society shifted from the earth, the animal and plant kingdoms, to the heavens, when the priestly watchers of the skies discovered that the seven celestial powers—sun, moon, and five visible planets—move at mathematically determinable rates through the fixed constellations."[6]

The point of interest here lies in the fact that thirty-five hundred years before Christ the Mesopotamians spoke of the sun, moon, and five visible planets as "the seven celestial powers." Is there a relationship between this concept and that of the seven spirit messengers in the Native American Medicine wheel?

Seven-ness

Arthur M. Young, in speaking of the cumulative nature of process, lists "This sequence of kingdoms:

> Light
>> Particles
>>> Atoms
>>>> Molecules
>>>>> Plants
>>>>>> Animals
>>>>>>> Man"

Young continues by saying that "Each kingdom, and each power, includes what has gone before and adds a contribution of its own. Each kingdom is a level of organization which depends on the one preceding."[7] Something in this form of logic sounds very much like the teachings from the Native American Medicine Wheel. Young titles his Appendix II "Seven-ness," and he treats the values of sevens in quantum theory, the seven postulates of projective geometry, and the heptaverton.[8]

Time and again we are discovering the importance of the number seven in many different cultures, both ancient and modern, and it primarily has to do with the concept of power in one form or another.

9

The Outer Circle
of Twelve Stones

Sun Bear's Vision

Some Medicine Wheel teachings come in sets of twelve. Sun Bear's vision of the Medicine Wheel takes the twelve stones of the outer circle and gives us what he calls an "earth astrology:" astrology in that it gives lessons about our birth totems from the twelve moons of the year. His vision gives us our animal, plant, and mineral totems for the moon under which we were born. This could aptly be called a "terraology." There are three moons in each of the four directions.

The following summary of Sun Bear's vision of these twelve stones is identical to my vision of this part of the Medicine Wheel:

The first of the three moons of the North is the earth renewal moon: December 22–January 19. The animal totem for this moon is the snow goose. The plant totem is the birch tree, and the mineral totem is the quartz. The color is white.

The second moon of the North is the rest and cleansing moon: January 20–February 18. The animal totem is the otter. The plant totem is the quaking aspen, and the mineral totem is silver. The color is silver.

The third moon of the North is the big winds moon:

February 19–March 20. The animal totem is the cougar. The plant totem is plantain, and the mineral totem is turquoise. The color is blue-green.

The first moon of the East is the budding trees moon: March 21–April 19. The animal totem is the red hawk. The plant totem is the dandelion, and the mineral totem is the fire opal. The color is yellow.

The second moon of the East is the frogs return moon: April 20–May 20. The animal totem is the beaver. The plant totem is the blue camas, and the mineral totem is chrysocolla. The color is blue.

The third moon of the East is the cornplanting moon: May 21–June 20. The animal totem is the deer. The plant totem is yarrow, and the mineral totem is the moss agate. The colors are white and green.

The first moon of the South is the strong sun moon: June 21–July 22. The animal totem is the flicker. The plant totem is the wild rose, and the mineral totem is the carnelian agate. The color is pink.

The second moon of the South is the ripe berries moon: July 23–August 22. The animal totem is the sturgeon. The plant totem is the raspberry, and the mineral totems are garnet and iron. The color is red.

The third moon of the South is the harvest moon: August 23–September 22. The animal totem is the brown bear. The plant totem is the violet, and the mineral totem is the amethyst. The color is purple.

The first moon of the West is the ducks fly moon: September 23–October 23. The animal totem is the raven. The plant totem is mullein, and the mineral totem is jasper. The color is brown.

The second moon of the West is the freeze up moon: October 24–November 21. The animal totem is the snake. The plant totem is the thistle, and the mineral totems are copper and malachite. The color is orange.

The third moon of the West is the long snows moon: November 22–December 21. The animal totem is the elk. The plant totem is the black spruce, and the mineral totem is obsidian. The color is black.

Sun Bear explains the meanings of these totems in his book *The Medicine Wheel—Earth Astrology.*[1]

Alcoholics Anonymous

Earlier we noted that each nation, state, county, city, and family as well as each individual is a Medicine Wheel. Organized groups are also Medicine Wheels.

Alcoholics Anonymous is a Medicine Wheel. Theirs is a simple but powerful Medicine Wheel with twelve stones in the outer circle, the realm of humans, and the center stone for the deity. These relate to each other in a powerful way. Many people have drawn upon the powers of this Medicine Wheel for their healing. The twelve stones in the outer wheel are the teachings of the Twelve Steps.

Medicine Wheels interlock with each other. The Twelve Steps relate to the teachings of the Sundance Medicine Wheel:

THE TWELVE STEPS OF ALCOHOLICS ANONYMOUS

1. We admitted we were powerless over alcohol—that our lives had become unmanageable.
2. Came to believe that a Power greater than ourselves could restore us to sanity.
3. Made a decision to turn our will and our lives over to the care of God as we understood Him.
4. Made a searching and fearless moral inventory of ourselves.
5. Admitted to God, to ourselves, and to another human being the exact nature of our wrongs.
6. Were entirely ready to have God remove all these defects of character.

7. Humbly asked Him to remove our shortcomings.
8. Made a list of all persons we had harmed, and became willing to make amends to them all.
9. Made direct amends to such people wherever possible, except when to do so would injure them or others.
10. Continued to take personal inventory and when we were wrong promptly admitted it.
11. Sought through prayer and meditation to improve our conscious contact with God as we understood Him, praying only for knowledge of His will for us and the power to carry that out.
12. Having had a spiritual awakening as the result of these steps, we tried to carry this message to alcoholics, and to practice these principles in all our affairs.

1. *We admitted we were powerless over alcohol—that our lives had become unmanageable.*

The Sundance Medicine Wheel teaching: We turn to the North with this one. Here we face the storm of the North named alcoholism. We acknowledge that we are facing this storm of alcoholism as we ask God the Spirit of the North to give us wisdom in this battle.

2. *Came to believe that a Power greater than ourselves could restore us to sanity.*

The Sundance Medicine Wheel teaching: Here our attention is focused on the center of the Medicine Wheel where the deity dwells, and we draw power from this central force that is really within us.

3. *Made a decision to turn our will and our lives over to the care of God as we understood Him.*

The Sundance Medicine Wheel teaching: Again we are turning to the Great Spirit in the center of our Medicine

Wheel. Let us remember that each of us is a Medicine Wheel; therefore we are turning to the power source that is within us.

4. *Made a searching and fearless moral inventory of ourselves.*

The Sundance Medicine Wheel teaching: Here we are turning to the West, the direction of the vision quest, the direction of introspection.

5. *Admitted to God, to ourselves, and to another human being the exact nature of our wrongs.*

The Sundance Medicine Wheel teaching is an interesting one. First, we turn to God at the altar in the center of the Medicine Wheel. Then we turn to ourselves and another human being in the outer circle, bringing the collective whole of this experience to bear upon the teachings of the West where we find cleansing and healing.

6. *Were entirely ready to have God remove all these defects of character.*

The Sundance Medicine Wheel teaching: Again we turn to God the Great Spirit centered within us, and to the West for cleansing and healing.

7. *Humbly asked Him to remove our shortcomings.*

The Sundance Medicine Wheel teaching: The Alcoholics Anonymous Medicine Wheel repeatedly returns to the importance of centering ourselves on the Great Spirit within us, and once again we turn to the West for cleansing and healing.

8. *Made a list of all persons we had harmed, and became willing to make amends to them all.*

The Sundance Medicine Wheel teaching: Now we turn to the North for the storms that we have caused to descend upon others, and follow that by turning to the West for healing. Through this action we can hope for forgiveness. At least we may be able to forgive ourselves.

9. *Made direct amends to such people wherever possible, except when to do so would injure them or others.*

The Sundance Medicine Wheel teaching: We are now solidly in the West, becoming a channel for the forces of healing to flow to others.

10. *Continued to take personal inventory and when we were wrong promptly admitted it.*

The Sundance Medicine Wheel teaching: We remain in the West in meditation and introspection, combining our discoveries about ourselves with the teachings of cleansing and healing.

11. *Sought through prayer and meditation to improve our conscious contact with God as we understood Him, praying only for knowledge of His will for us and the power to carry that out.*

The Sundance Medicine Wheel teaching: The West is the direction for prayer and meditation. It is interesting to note here that while we are in the darkness of the West we are facing the incoming light from the East that is bringing knowledge and enlightenment into our world of darkness.

12. *Having had a spiritual awakening as the result of these steps, we tried to carry this message to alcoholics, and to practice these principles in all our affairs.*

The Sundance Medicine Wheel teaching: Here we make the entire cycle, beginning with the spiritual awakening in the East, allowing it to grow and develop in the South, bringing healing in the West as we carry the message to alcoholics, and coming to the culmination of the cycle in the North as we practice all of these principles in our lives. This is a good Medicine Wheel. We should note that most of the action takes place in the West, the direction of healing. Healing is what we are seeking, but this wheel also ends with excellent balance by making the entire cycle in all four directions.

10

The Circles
as a Calendar

The Model

The center stone is always today. The seven stones immediately around the center stone are the seven days of the week. The four directions are the four weeks of the month, and the twelve stones in the outer wheel are the twelve months of the year. We now have a complete calendar, but how will it facilitate providing a way to reveal the Medicine Wheel teachings to us in a powerful manner?

You are about to enter the most profound part of this journey. We now enter into the spiraling of all the teachings. You will now prepare to consider each of the twelve totems of the outer wheel as they may be understood in each of the powers of the four directions through the eyes of each of the seven spirit messengers of the inner circle. Remember that all of this is within you and not outside of you, for you are the wheel and the wheel is you!

The Discovery

You shall soon discover that this calendar will provide you with an important daily devotional guide. The twelve months of the year or the twelve moons are:

December 22—January 19; snow goose is the animal totem.
January 20–February 18; otter is the animal totem.
February 19–March 20; cougar is the animal totem.
March 21–April 19; hawk is the animal totem.
April 20–May 20; beaver is the animal totem.
May 21–June 20; deer is the animal totem.
June 21–July 22; flicker is the animal totem.
July 23–August 22; sturgeon is the animal totem.
August 23–September 22; bear is the animal totem.
September 23–October 23; raven is the animal totem.
October 24–November 21; snake is the animal totem.
November 22–December 21; elk is the animal totem.

On the first day of each moon the animal totem will be yellow, reflecting the teachings of the East, and will remain in that direction and that color for the seven days of that week. That animal totem will then move to the South where it will become white, reflecting the teachings of that direction. The third week of that moon it will be black in the West, and the fourth and final week it will be red in the North. On the first day of each week you should meditate on how you see that particular animal in the teachings of the East through the eyes of the Spirit Messenger owl, the second day through the eyes of the cougar, and the third day through the hawk's eyes. The fourth day will be the coyote's turn to speak to you about that animal in the East, while on the fifth day it will be the wolf's revelation. The bear gets in on the act on the sixth day, and the raven concludes the week on the seventh day.

The next week you will go through the same seven spirit messengers with that month's animal totem as white in the South. The third week your animal totem will be understood by these Spirit Messengers while it is black in the West, and the fourth and final week of the month while your animal totem is red in the North.

On the first day of the next new moon you will begin the same process with the next animal totem.

Let us suppose that as you are now reading this you realize that the next new moon will begin August 23. Your animal totem will be the bear. Throughout the first week you will recognize the spirit of the bear within you as yellow. Meditate on how you visualize a yellow bear in the teachings of the East through the eyes of the owl. The next day consider the bear through your understanding of the cougar. The third day you listen to the hawk talk to you about your yellow bear, and the fourth day the coyote gets to do some trickster teaching for you. The wolf speaks to you on the fifth day, and on the sixth day the bear looks at herself and tells you how she feels about herself as a yellow bear in the East. The raven concludes the week with her unveilings of the yellow bear of the East within you.

On the second week of that moon, the bear becomes white in the South, and each day you consider how the spirit messenger of that day sees the white bear of the South within you. The third week the bear is black in the West and the fourth week she becomes red in the North.

On the first day of the next new moon you will begin the same process all over again with a yellow raven in the East. This approach could provide many powerful insights regarding yourself during the course of the year. It could become a marvelous energy giver by helping you to find a new sense of balance in your life. It should help you to remain centered. While these daily meditations will become a guide through which you will be able to soar high philosophically and theologically, they will also help you to remain well grounded. Try it!!

11

The Four Paths to the Sacred Altar

There are four paths to the sacred altar in the Sundance Medicine Wheel.

The four doors to these paths are the four sons of the Great Spirit: the buffalo, which is sacramental; the bear, which speaks of service; the eagle, which is incarnational; and the cougar, which leads us into our search for truth (see Figure 18).

cougar

eagle

sacred altar

buffalo

Figure 18.

bear

The adventure on each of these paths is not only linear but also spatial. We encounter a linear experience as we progress from one animal totem to the next, but life is actually more complex than that. On many occasions we experience all of the totems on a given event in life. This then becomes a spatial experience with both horizontal and vertical spiritual experiences; horizontal in giving us time consciousness to the event, and vertical in compounding the spiritual energy.

The Path from the East

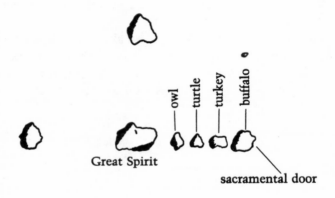

Great Spirit

owl · turtle · turkey · buffalo

sacramental door

Figure 19.

The Buffalo
The buffalo, in the East, opens the sacramental door (see Figure 19). This is an important door through which to travel in order to discover and experience the Great Spirit, or God. God becomes sacramental to humankind, thus teaching us that we must learn to give ourselves back to

God as a sacrament. We begin our journey on this path by first observing the buffalo. The buffalo is a giver. The buffalo gave its hide to our ancestors to provide them with shelter, and gave its meat for food. The buffalo gave its hooves for glue, and its sinew for thread. The soft buffalo robes kept our people warm in the winters. Every part of the buffalo was used. The buffalo gave itself completely. The buffalo was a perfect, complete potlatch. Through the gift of the buffalo the Creator taught us that the Great Spirit is prepared to meet all of our needs. We are also taught that we must reciprocate and learn to give our all.

Ancient tribal Judaism taught that "You shall love the Lord your God with all your heart, and with all your soul, and with all your might" (Deuteronomy 6:5, RSV). These tribal people made many ritualistic sacrifices at the door of their tabernacle as they traveled across the wilderness. One of those sacrifices was known as "the burnt offering," during which the ox (buffalo) was completely consumed or sacrificed. The Creator became a sacrament by giving of the Divine Self completely, and now we enter the sacramental door by learning to give our lives as a sacrament back to the Creator.

Jesus said that it is better to give than to receive. He ultimately gave of himself completely at the center flowering tree of Calvary. He became our sacrament, our buffalo, the ancient tribal Jew's ox. Many Christians seem to believe that the ceremony ends when they partake of the Eucharist in the sanctuary, when, in fact, the ritual has just begun. They should now become the Eucharist as they leave the sanctuary and journey out into their community. They should become a living sacrament—a living sacrifice. Paul said, "I appeal to you therefore, brethren, by the mercies of God, to present your bodies as a living sacrifice, holy and acceptable to God, which is your spiritual worship" (Romans 12:1, RSV).

The Turkey EAST

As we continue down this path from the East we come next to the turkey. Many Native Americans speak of the turkey as the Give-Away Eagle. The turkey sacrifices itself so that we may live. The turkey is the winged example of buffalo. It performs the ritual of the potlatch or give-away ceremony. We learn that life is sacred through the buffalo and the turkey as we walk the sacramental path toward the sacred altar where we may experience God the Great Spirit.

The Turtle EAST

The next lesson that we learn on the journey of this path is from the turtle. The turtle is symbolic of our Earth Mother. We speak of the earth as "Turtle Island." All of creation comes from the dust of our Earth Mother, and to the dust we shall all one day return. We are born from the womb of our Earth Mother. The turtle reminds us that as we have received, so must we also give. We must give back to our Earth Mother as she has given to us. She has been sacramental to us, and we must become sacramental to her. This means that we must become a living sacrament to all life. We must learn to give ourselves to others.

The buffalo, turkey, and turtle are great medicine powers. There is much to experience about the Great Spirit God when we walk this pathway. Those persons who are totally dependent upon others can never experience the rewards of this pathway's medicine powers. Those who are totally independent are also rejecting this pathway. This is the pathway of inter-dependency, of giving and receiving. Some people may be heard to make the remark that they are waiting for their ship to come in, but the question may be asked of them, "Have you ever sent your ship out?" After all, it cannot return unless you have sent it out. The garden will not grow unless you have planted the seed. The sacramental path is an important and powerful way to journey.

The Owl EAST

Experiencing the journey from the buffalo through the turkey and the turtle will bring us to the medicine power of the owl. We are drawing very near to the sacred altar as we approach the owl. The owl, who has such acute vision in the darkness of the night, allows us to see beyond the sacred altar into the darkness of the West. Experiencing the buffalo, turkey, and turtle gives us a greater understanding of God and a better perception of the sacred mysteries that lie ahead of us. This is owl medicine. This is the Spirit searching the deep things of God and revealing them unto us. Certain mysteries of life are only revealed to those who unreservedly and without hesitation walk the sacramental path.

The Path from the South

The Bear SOUTH

The bear, in the South, opens the door to service (see Figure 20). The bear medicine power is made manifest through the warriors, the healers, and the leaders. Bear people live to give service to their respective communities. Much can only be experienced and learned about God by dedicating oneself to a life of service. Jesus said, "Whosoever will be chief among you, let him be your servant" (Matthew 20:27, KJ).

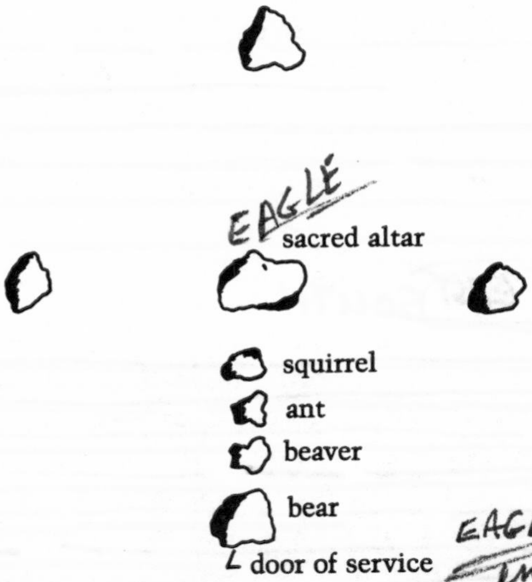

Family Reunion

EAGLE
sacred altar

squirrel

ant

beaver

Figure 20.

bear

door of service

EAGLE Incarnation Door

The Beaver South

Continuing on this path from the South we come next to the beaver. It is important to learn beaver medicine in order to encounter God on this path of service. The beaver is industrious, and a person who is going to serve must be a diligent person. Such a person needs beaver medicine power. The beaver never stops growing, and people who walk the pathway of service must continue to grow and develop in their area of responsibility. The beaver is an engineer. This is a pathway of creativity, and with beaver medicine power we learn to design new ways to achieve or accomplish the Great Spirit's goals. The beaver can build a series of dams connecting them with canals in which they control the flow of water through locks. On this pathway of service to the Creator, people learn to manage and control their time and energies.

The Ant South

The next lesson we learn on the journey of this path is from the ant. The ant can carry loads many times its own weight, and over great distances. The ant and beaver have one thing in common—they are both builders. The ant patiently and deliberately continues to persevere in its building program. As we add the medicine powers of the ant to those of the beaver and bear, we discover that we are drawing ever closer to the sacred altar.

The Squirrel SOUTH

The final lessons we learn on this path are from the squirrel. The squirrel is a gatherer. With squirrel medicine power a person gathers all he or she has learned from the bear, beaver, and ant and plans ahead for the tough winter that is coming. With squirrel medicine one is always prepared for one's obligations of service to the Great Spirit in one's community.

The pathway of service is an exciting and beautiful adventure in getting acquainted with God the Great Spirit.

The Path from the West

The Eagle WEST

The eagle, in the West, opens the door to incarnation (see Figure 21). The eagle is the symbol for the Great Spirit, or God, at the sacred altar in the center of the wheel. The eagle is also here in the outer circle of humanity at the door from the West. This reveals to us that the deity in the center of the circle has become incarnate in humanity at the outer circle. God dwells in human beings. Divinity resides within each of us. We begin our walk down this path to get better acquainted with our divine parent as a member of the divine family. This is the path to our divine family reunion. In 1 Corinthians 3: 16, Paul said that we should know that the Spirit of God dwells within us. John

Returning Home!

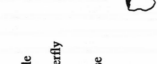

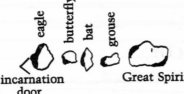

incarnation
door

Great Spirit

Figure 21.

informs us that we are children of God. We are family!
The Medicine Wheel teaches us this great truth also.

The Butterfly   WEST

The butterfly has lessons for us as we continue our journey
down this pathway. We go through stages of transformation as we travel down this path from the outer circle of
humanity toward the dwelling place of our divine home.
As the butterfly moves from the egg stage to the larva
stage and through the cocoon stage to the birth stage, even
so we move through stages of spiritual transformation in
the process of becoming aware of the Great Spirit's incarnation within us. In the cocoon stage we concentrate inward. We have learned that this is a teaching of the West.
It is here that we will discover the God within us. Many
people make this discovery at the time of their vision
quest, and as we mentioned earlier, this takes place in the
western direction of the Medicine Wheel.

The Bat WEST

Continuing down the path we meet the bat. The bat embraces the concept of spirit death and rebirth. The bat hangs upside-down in its cave and becomes a symbol of the transformation of the old self into a new creation. The darkness of the cave is like the darkness of the grave or of the mother's womb. We died in that former existence in our mother's womb and we were born into this time of awareness.

The sweatlodge is a symbol of this experience. We take our entire universe with us into the sweatlodge and are reminded of being in the womb of the Great Spirit. When we leave the sweatlodge we leave the "old man," or the old self-nature, behind us in the lodge as we are "born-again." We become a new creature. We are more aware of the experience of incarnation that is taking place within us.

The vision quest is another place in which we become aware of the incarnation taking place. We are never the same after we encounter the Great Spirit in the vision quest. Traditionally, in many tribes, boys go on their first vision quest at the age of puberty. This becomes a rite of passage from boyhood into manhood. They leave the boy behind them and come out having experienced their birth into manhood.

Paul speaks of this idea of the burial of the old man, or old self, in the waters of Christian baptism and rising to walk in newness of life in Romans chapter 6.

The Grouse WEST

The journey down this path from the eagle door through the butterfly and the bat eventually brings us to the grouse. The grouse will teach you the spiral dance, the dance of birth and rebirth. This sacred spirit whirlwind will take you to the center—the sacred altar. You have given birth to the Great Spirit within you. This should be a daily experience. Throughout the sacred spiral dance we transcend to higher stages of awareness of the God that is within us.

The Path from the North

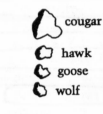

cougar

hawk

goose

wolf

sacred altar

Figure 22.

The Cougar NORTH

The cougar, in the North, opens the door to the search (see Figure 22). The cougar climbs higher than any other member of the cat family. The spirit of the cougar leads us into the theological and philosophical heights on this pathway of searching for truth and knowledge. The cougar also feels very much at home on the earth, and therefore helps us to become well grounded with our newly discovered truths. This opens the door for us to begin our journey in search of truth.

The Hawk ~~NORTH~~

Next is the hawk, who flies very high. The only winged that flies higher is the eagle. Many tribes call the hawk the little eagle. The hawk has great vision medicine power, and helps us to see things that others cannot see. This is the medicine power of insight. The hawk is a great hunter, and this medicine power aids us in our hunt or search for knowledge and wisdom. Many tribes use the hawk's feathers in healing ceremonies. It is this medicine power that heals us of old concepts which have been injurious. According to both Old Testament Judaism and New Testament Christianity, this is the office and work of the Holy Spirit.

The Goose NORTH

As we proceed we encounter the goose. The cougar and the hawk can help us with our sense of perception, vision, and insight, but the goose is the one with long flight endurance. The goose can fly up to five thousand miles from its northern nesting grounds to the Gulf of Mexico. We need this medicine power of endurance in our quest for truth. Many times we are aware that we are onto something, but we give up too soon and never discover the pearl we are looking for. Goose medicine empowers us for a long flight in our quest.

The Wolf NORTH

The cougar, hawk, and goose eventually lead us to the wolf. The wolf is the pathfinder and protector. The wolf directs us on our path to the sacred altar and God the Great Spirit. The wolf also protects us from incorrect or negative teachings while we are on our quest. This is what Jesus was speaking of when he asked: "What father among you, if his son asks for a fish, will instead of a fish give him a serpent; or if he asks for an egg, will give him a scorpion? If you then, who are evil, know how to give good gifts to your children, how much more will the heavenly Father give the Holy Spirit to those who ask him?" (Luke 11:11–13, RSV).

Summary

You will recall the legend of how the Great Spirit divided his powers among his four sons. We also remember that we need to experience all four of these powers in order for us to have a well-balanced relationship with the Creator. We therefore need to enter all four of these doors: the sacramental door, the door of service, the incarnation door, and the door that opens to our questing journey. We need to walk all four of these paths each day. Anyone who will dare to do so intentionally will live a very exciting and beautiful life. You will discover that upon awakening in the morning you will be tingling with excitement, wondering what the Creator has in store for you that day.

Great Spirit gave
4 Sons powers
we need to experience
all of these powers in
order for us to have
well balanced
relationship with the
creator. Therefore ENTER
ALL 4 Doors N, S, E, W
walk all 4 every day.

Part IV

*The Red Road
and the
Black Road*

Medicine wheel
Red - Sacred Color) life
ETERNAL Life (of today)
Black - Color **12** *night (of blood)*
darkness
where we get lost :
Life of DISTRUCTION

The Red Road and Black Road Medicine Wheel

There are many different Medicine Wheels. In the previous chapters we have been studying the Sundance Medicine Wheel. In the Red and Black Road Medicine Wheel we see the four directions as two roads. The North-South direction is entirely red, and is known as the Red Road. The West-East direction is black, and is known as the Black Road. The Red Road represents the balanced life and is the good road. The Black Road represents the unbalanced life and is the bad road. All of us are constantly on one of these two roads, and we have all walked on both. There are days when we spend time walking on each of these roads.

This Medicine Wheel existed among my people long before white, black, or yellow people ever came to the shores of this land. We had never met people of these other colors, and these two colors do not refer to the red and black races. The understanding of these colors in this Medicine Wheel is to be realized in red as the sacred color of life. It is the color of blood; it is life. We wrap our sacred objects in red cloth. These are our sacred bundles. Black is the color of the night. It is easy to get lost in the darkness of the night without any light.

The great medicine man, Jesus, talked about these two roads. He spoke of them as the narrow road and the broad road. He said that the narrow road leads to eternal life, and that the broad road leads to death and destruction. He did not elaborate on these teachings, but we can learn more about what he was speaking of by studying this Medicine Wheel. It is a good commentary on his teachings.

All of us are very close to the center, the intersection of these two roads, regardless of the road we are presently traveling. And who is at the very center? The intersection is the place of the sacred altar, the dwelling place of the Great Spirit, or God. God is at the intersection of the two roads. The intersection of these two roads is identical to the intersection in the center of the Sundance Medicine Wheel. Some may ask, "How far can I get from the center or from God? How close can I get to the edge of the circle?" We approach the edge of the circle only at the time of death. Otherwise we are always very close to the center. The teaching that some people are far from God is very misleading. Some church hymns speak of people drifting far from God, and there has been too much erroneous preaching of this kind. Consequently, many people have believed this repulsive, destructive concept and never turn to the God that is within them. The same church that preaches about our being able to be far from God also preaches the omnipresence of that same God. How can I ever be in a place in which an omnipresent God is not? This is Impossible! David, the Psalmist said: "If I make my bed in hell, behold, thou art there" (Psalms 139:8, KJ). We can never get away from God, and God can never get away from us. God dwells within every human being.

In our Native American theology we might ask, "Where is the center of the earth?" We are not asking for the geographical center of the earth but the spiritual center. The center of the earth is within you. It is within me. That is the Medicine Wheel teaching. Jesus said that the kingdom does not come with observation, it is neither here nor there, but that the kingdom lies within you. That is the Medicine Wheel teaching also. How far west can you go before you run out of West? Remember, this is circular spirituality and not a square theology. No matter how far you may travel you will never run out of West. You will still have as much before you as when you began. The same is true for any of the four directions. Why? Because you took the center with you. The center lies within you. And who is always at that center? Look at your Medicine Wheel. The Creator, the Great Spirit, God is always at the center. The omnipresent God is always within all of us.

An Indian teaching is that an Indian is never alone, Creator God is always with us. God says, "I will never leave thee, nor forsake thee" (Heb. 13:5, KJ). Jesus said, "Lo, I am with you always, to the close of the age" (Matt. 28:20, RSV). Jesus believed in a good Native American theological concept. Others would say that Native American theology has a good Christological center. Either way, we must remain centered for good spiritual health. The fact that we are always near the center does not mean that we remain centered. We may be at the center but have our backs turned toward it. We may be ignoring the Great Spirit within us. Isaiah speaks of this when he says that "We hid as it were our faces from him" (Isaiah 52:3, KJ). This is a picture of a person who has turned his or her back on the center, but who is now looking back over his or her shoulder to that center. This is the beginning of the act of centering ourselves on the Great Spirit who is always within us at the crossroads of life.

So, we are all on one of the two roads, and we are all close to the center. This close proximity to the center is what causes much stress and tension. Some members of a family try walking the Red Road, while others walk the Black Road of alcohol and drug abuse, or other ways. It is within the stress and tension of this close relationship that we learn many of life's lessons. We become knowledgeable so that we may be able to help our brothers and sisters on the Black Road to find their way to the Red Road. None of us walks the Red Road consistently. All of us have experienced walking the unbalanced life. We cannot afford to be judgmental, only supportive and nurturing. Walking the Red Road should always be our goal.

Medicine Wheels interlock with each other on many, many occasions. The teachings that go with the stress and tension teachings of this Medicine Wheel interrelate with the storm teachings of the North in the Sundance Medicine Wheel.

Remember, the Creator is always at the center, very close to us, always ready to help us. We need only to knock, ask, seek. To be aware of the center we need to remain centered, focused.

Another teaching in this Medicine Wheel is about the spirits of our ancestors. While we are walking the Red Road, they are on the Black Road. This does not mean that they are walking a life out of balance, but rather, they are on a plane of which we are not consciously aware most of the time. They are continuously around us, their spirits whispering to our spirits. It has been estimated that some 40 percent of the people have experienced departed loved ones' returning to commune with them.

The story of Saul visiting the medium of Endor in order to communicate with departed Samuel is an example of this relationship (1 Samuel 28:6–14). Although Samuel did not desire to be disturbed, instances of departed spirits' returning to loved ones is quite common.

Part V

Other Medicine Wheels

13

Other Indian Medicine Wheels

Hyemeyohsts Storm's Wheel

The book *Seven Arrows*, written by Hyemeyohsts Storm, gives a very thorough understanding of the Medicine Wheel. Much of the book is a telling of the old stories, or legends, but all of these are told to help one understand the Medicine Wheel in a traditional way. I have taken these Medicine Wheel teachings and attempted to build bridges between our traditional Native American spirituality and the other religions and cultures of the world, both ancient and modern.

Hyemeyohsts Storm talks about the differences in our perceptions as we sit in a circle and view an object in the center. He talks about levels upon levels of perspectives we must consider. He not only suggests what happens when we put a feather or drum in the center but also describes how much more complex our perspectives become when we put an abstraction there, "such as an idea, a feeling, or a philosophy."[1] He speaks of the Medicine Wheel as being a mirror in which everything is reflected—not only the entire universe that is out there but also the universe that is within you.

The Medicine Wheel he presents is the one that gives the sundance teaching. He says that a child's first teaching is of the Four Great Powers. However, his colors of the four directions are different from those of the other teachers as shown on the chart in Chapter 2. There is no conflict between his teachings and theirs; rather, he adds much depth to our understanding of the Sundance Medicine Wheel.

The Sweatlodge Medicine Wheel

The sweatlodge is a powerful Medicine Wheel. It is built in the form of a circle. When we enter the sweatlodge we sit in the positions of the stones in the outer circle. The sacred altar is in the center—the dwelling place of the Great Spirit. God the Great Spirit speaks to us out of the fire in the sacred altar. We take our entire universe into the sweatlodge with us. We sing and we pray in the sweatlodge, and there we find healing, insights, spiritual growth, empowerment. We leave our "old person" behind as we leave the sweatlodge womb of the Great Spirit and find that we are born anew, or "born again." Everything that we have been saying about the Medicine Wheel can take place within the sweatlodge. It is a powerful Medicine Wheel.

The Wheel of Life

Some people refer to the Medicine Wheel as the Wheel of Life. You cannot find the point of beginning or the point of ending to the circle. It is the symbol of eternal life. The Medicine Wheel vision taught us long ago that we can

have a hope in eternal life. Everything that we experience
in life can be found in the Medicine Wheel.

The Sacred Hoop

The Great Spirit not only dwells in the center of the Medicine Wheel but also reaches out to the fullness of the outer
circle. The Medicine Wheel takes in the entire universe,
and everything in the universe is sacred. As Native American people we cannot separate the sacred from the secular.
There is no separation of church and state in our old traditional ways. The clan, the village, the tribe, the people are
sacred. I am the village, and the village is me—I am sacred.
The Great Spirit is in all things, and all things are in the
Great Spirit. We are panentheists.

This is the Christian doctrine of the omnipresence of
God that most Christians do not understand. They claim
that they believe in this doctrine, but they live a life in
direct contradiction to what they claim to believe. If God
is everywhere, then that God must dwell in all things,
including all people. The Augustinian doctrine of original
sin prevails in both the Catholic and the Protestant
Church. Christians claim that the scripture teaches us
that in Adam all die, but evidently they do not read the
remainder of that verse which says, "so also in Christ shall
all be made alive" (1 Cor. 15:22, RSV). Why is it that we
pick up on the "all" in the first part of that verse, and not
on the "all" of the latter part? If we can believe in universal death because of the first "all" in the verse, why can
we not believe in universal salvation because of the second
"all" in the verse? The Western Christian understanding
here has placed Christians in an anthropocentric prison.
Salvation becomes one of the inner soul rather than that
of all creation as it should be understood. When we come

to this biblical understanding, then everything becomes sacred as our Native American Medicine Wheel has always taught us. Divinity dwells within every one of us. Everything is sacred. I am a Medicine Wheel, a Sacred Hoop. You are a Medicine Wheel, a Sacred Hoop.

The Nation's Hoop

We have said that every nation is a Medicine Wheel. Black Elk, in relating his great vision, tells of how he looked and "saw that in nearly every tepee the women and the children and the men lay dying with the dead.

"So I rode around the circle of the village, looking in upon the sick and dead, and I felt like crying as I rode. But when I looked behind me, all the women and the children and the men were getting up and coming forth with happy faces.

"And a Voice said: 'Behold, they have given you the center of the nation's hoop to make it live!' "[2]

Black Elk saw his nation as a Sacred Hoop with himself at the center as its redeeming force. Thus he saw the Great Spirit incarnate within him redeeming the people of his nation.

Black Elk also related that as he walked alone, he "heard the sun singing as it arose, and it sang like this:

'With visible face I am appearing.
In a sacred manner I appear.
For the greening earth a pleasantness I make.
The center of the nation's hoop I have made pleasant.
With visible face behold me!
The four-leggeds and two-leggeds, I have made them
  to walk;
The wings of the air, I have made them to fly.

With visible face I appear.
My day, I have made it holy.' "³

This could be a psalm sung by that ancient tribal person, David the Israelite. We might call it Black Elk's Psalm of the Nation's Hoop.

The Sundance Ceremony as a Medicine Wheel

The Sundance Ceremony is a very powerful Medicine Wheel. The people gather in the outer circle under the arbor—the place of all humanity. The center flowering tree, in the very center of the circle, is the sacred altar— the dwelling place of the Great Spirit, or God. The inner circle, the place of the powerful spirit messengers, is where we find the sundancers who are tethered to the Great Spirit in the sacred altar of the flowering tree. There is another circle between the sundancers and the prayer supporters in the arbor. This is a circle of many prayer sticks that are painted the colors of the four directions. Between this circle of prayer sticks and the sundancers is a circle of committed prayer supporters who have spent much time in preparations for this sundance through sweatlodges and fasting.

This is a death and resurrection Medicine Wheel, very similar to Calvary—the center flowering tree to which Jesus was tethered and danced his sundance.

14

◈◈◈

Non-Indian Medicine Wheels

There are many ancient Medicine Wheels. Every ancient culture had its Medicine Wheel. It is interesting to see how these interrelate with the Native American Medicine Wheels.

Thoth Hermes Trismegistus

Hermes was regarded by the ancient Egyptians as the embodiment of the universal mind. Notice how very closely his vision relates to our Native American Sundance Medicine Wheel:

> The man longed to pierce the circumference of the circles and understand the mystery of Him who sat upon the eternal fire. Having already all power, He stooped down and peeped through the seven harmonies and, breaking through the strength of the circles, made Himself manifest to Nature stretched out below. The Man, looking into the depths, smiled, for He beheld a shadow upon the earth and a likeness mirrored in the waters, which shadow and likeness were a reflection of Himself. The Man fell in love with His own shadow and desired to descend into it. Coincident with the desire, the intelligent thing united itself with the unreasoning image or shape.
>
> Nature, beholding the descent, wrapped herself

about the Man whom she loved, and the two were mingled. For this reason, earthy man is composite. Within him is the Sky Man, immortal and beautiful; without is nature, mortal and destructible. Thus suffering is the result of the Immortal Man's falling in love with His shadow and giving up reality to dwell in the darkness of illusion; for, being immortal, man has the power of the Seven Governors—also the Life, the Light, the Word—but being mortal, he is controlled by the rings of the Governors—Fate or Destiny.[4]

Hermes sees the multiple circles with the deity in the center with the eternal fire just as it is in our Native American Medicine Wheel. He recognizes the seven harmonies or Seven Governors (Spirit Messengers), and that the Medicine Wheel mirrors life. He also sees what we call the "Mitakoye Oyasin" in that both nature and man are one, that they are mingled, and that man is indwelt with divinity, for within him is the immortal sky man. The ancient Egyptians understood our Native American Medicine Wheel.

The Chinese Zodiac

The Chinese Zodiac is also a wheel with twelve important points. This wheel consists of a twelve-year cycle. Each year is named after a different animal that imparts distinct characteristics to its year. Many Chinese believe that the year of a person's birth is the primary factor in determining that person's personality traits, physical and mental attributes, and degree of success and happiness throughout his or her lifetime. To learn about your animal sign, find the year of your birth among the twelve signs. If you were born before 1943 or after 1990, add or subtract twelve to find your year.

1. Rabbit—1951, 1963, 1975, 1987. Luckiest of all signs, you are also talented and articulate. Affectionate, yet shy, you seek peace throughout your life.

2. Dragon—1952, 1964, 1976, 1988. You are eccentric and your life is complex. You have a very passionate nature and abundant health.

3. Snake—1953, 1965, 1977, 1989. Wise and intense with a tendency toward physical beauty. Vain and high tempered.

4. Horse—1954, 1966, 1978, 1990. Popular and attractive to the opposite sex. You are often ostentatious and impatient. You need people.

5. Sheep—1943, 1955, 1967, 1979. Elegant and creative. You are timid and prefer anonymity.

6. Monkey—1944, 1956, 1968, 1980. You are very intelligent and are able to influence people. An enthusiastic achiever, you are easily discouraged and confused.

7. Cock—1945, 1957, 1969, 1981. A pioneer in spirit, you are devoted to work and quest after knowledge. You are selfish and eccentric.

8. Dog—1946, 1958, 1970, 1982. Loyal and honest, you work well with others. You are generous yet stubborn and often selfish.

9. Boar—1947, 1959, 1971, 1983. Noble and chivalrous. Your friends will be lifelong, yet you are prone to marital strife.

10. Rat—1948, 1960, 1972, 1984. You are ambitious yet honest. You are prone to spend freely. You seldom make lasting friendships.

11. Ox—1949, 1961, 1973, 1985. Bright, patient, and inspiring to others. You can be happy by yourself, yet you make an outstanding parent.

12. Tiger—1950, 1962, 1974, 1986. Tiger people are aggressive, courageous, candid and sensitive.

The Chinese Zodiac has been included in this study in order that we might see how another ancient culture viewed life as being cyclical, with twelve important points in the outer wheel and with animals as being symbolic of human personality traits.

Stonehenge

Stonehenge is probably the best known of some forty to fifty prehistoric circular monuments in the British Isles. These ruins are located on the Salisbury Plain in southern England. This was an important religious center from approximately 1900 to 1400 B.C.

Historically its construction took place in three stages. The first stage was between 1900 and 1700 B.C. The second period was from about 1700 to 1500 B.C., and the third and final phase took place at about 1500 to 1400 B.C. Many writers believed that it was built by the Druids, but we now know that the Druids did not come to Britain until about one thousand years after Stonehenge was abandoned. Who built Stonehenge is still a mystery.

There has been much speculation as to its original function. Was it purely a religious structure? Was it built by the scientists of that day to assist them in their study of astronomy? It was built with an orientation to the sun and its solstices. Could it have included a little of both religion and astronomy?

Native Americans have no difficulty seeing that this is an ancient Medicine Wheel. The center of the circle is most certainly a sacred altar, and the wheels within the wheels all had deep spiritual significance to the people who built it. They not only worshiped at this place but Stonehenge was like their Bible—it taught them their lessons about life.

all teach us lessons on how to live.

12 Stones) 12 months / of year / w/ animal . et 12 s
w/ animal . et 12 s
Totems

7 Messengers
7 angels
7 lamp stands
etc 7.

4 Apostles } Matthew
Mark
4 directions Luke
N, S, E, W John.
4 Pathways to
Sacred altar :

} 4 paths to
Sacred altar
daily
ritual
way of life

Summary
and Conclusion

Summary

We began by comparing three visions: the Native American Medicine Wheel vision, John the Apostle's vision and Ezekiel's vision. We discovered numerous ways to cycle the teachings of the four directions after having studied them individually. The inner circle of the seven spirit messengers then became the center of our focus. This was followed by teachings from the outer wheel of twelve stones.

We encountered the spiraling of these compounded teachings in the combined circles as a calendar that provides us with a daily Medicine Wheel guide to which we can bring our life experiences. The Wheel then becomes a mirror and reflects back to us new insights as a guide for our lives.

Next we walked the four paths to the sacred altar. This should become a daily ritual—a way of life!

We then climaxed the study with a brief look at the Red

Road and Black Road Medicine Wheel along with a few other Indian as well as non-Indian Medicine Wheels.

Conclusion

Now that you have reached this point in the book, you may be asking the question: "Where do I go from here?"

This is not the end of this quest. This is only the beginning. I have presented a basic comparative study revealing relationships between my Native American spirituality and that of Judaism and Christianity, with a little sprinkling of a few other ancient concepts. The Medicine Wheel encourages you to continue this exciting journey by adding insights from your spiritual life experience, whether that may be of Christianity, Buddhism, Islam, or any other. We need to continue looking for the many other relationships that exist. The Creator has revealed herself to all people in all cultures throughout the entire catalogue of the human race.

The Medicine Wheel also urges you to bring your own personal life experiences to it. Allow the Wheel to act as a mirror to this diary of events. These personal life experiences may come from your own rites of passage, or from encounters in your family life. They might be experiences you have entertained in your larger circle of social awareness.

Allow the Medicine Wheel to become a daily mirror to your life. Begin each day pondering the teachings of the Wheel as you turn to the East and begin your prayer time to the Creator in each of the four directions.

Always attempt to remain well centered as you endeavor to walk the Red Road. Allow yourself to soar high spiritually or theologically as well as philosophically, and yet be ever mindful of the necessity to remain well grounded.

It would be advisable for you to reread this book. A second reading should reveal more to you regarding your attempt to walk a balanced life. It will help to give you new insights. A second reading will provide you with the opportunity to begin building upon the foundation of the first reading.

Would you like to continue learning more about Native American spirituality? I recommend that you begin by reading some of the books in the bibliography of this work.

Find a talking circle group that you can meet with regularly. Begin attending pow-wows. Find a sweatlodge that you may go to regularly. Prepare to go on a vision quest. Bring your life experience to Native American spirituality, and allow Native American spirituality to penetrate your past cultural experiences. Allow them to enhance and empower each other.

Take these ancient teachings into your life. Let the Medicine Wheel speak to you as it has to those before you and as it shall to those who will follow you.

Glossary

Anthropocentric: Regarding humankind as being the central fact of the universe. This is humankind turned inward on itself.

Carnelian: A reddish stone of the variety of chalcedony.

Eclectic: One who selects or chooses doctrines or methods from various sources or systems.

Eschatology: The doctrines of the last or final things.

Exclusivist: One who excludes someone else because he or she does nòt believe the same as the exclusivist.

Fundamentalist: One who believes in the inerrancy of the Bible as fundamental to Christianity.

Jasper: An opaque, uncrystalline variety of quartz.

Mandala: A sacred shield.

Mitakoye Oyasin: Sioux Indian words meaning "All my relatives," or "We are all related."

Panentheism: The belief that God is *in* all things, and that all things are *in* God.

Panentheist: One who believes in panentheism.

Pantheist: One who believes that God is all things and that all things are God.

Potlatch: A Native American give-away ceremony celebrated for many different reasons.

Proselytization: The practice of making converts from another belief system.

Tamanawas: Salish Indian concept of a person's Medicine Spirit or Spirit Guide.

Vision Quest: A time of fasting and prayer, usually on a mountain, seeking one's Tamanawas or Spirit Guide.

Notes

Introduction

1. Ed McGaa, *Mother Earth Spirituality* (San Francisco: Harper & Row, 1989), p. 158.
2. Tom Brown, Jr., *The Vision* (New York: Berkley Books, 1988), p. 3.

Chapter 2

1. John G. Neihardt, *Black Elk Speaks* (New York, Pocket Books: 1959), p. 2.
2. John (Fire) Lame Deer and Richard Erdoes, *Lame Deer: Seeker of Visions* (New York: Pocket Books, 1976), p. 178.
3. Hyemeyohsts Storm, *Seven Arrows* (New York: Ballantine Books, 1972), p. 6.
4. Ron Zeilinger, *Sacred Ground* (Chamberlain, S.D.: Tipi Press, n.d.) pp. 50, 51.

Chapter 3

1. T. C. McLuhan, *Touch the Earth, A Self-Portrait of Indian Existence* (New York: Pocket Books, 1972), p. 36.
2. Many of these teachings of the East can be found in: Judie Bopp, Michael Bopp, Lee Brown, and Phil Lane, *The Sacred Tree*, Lethbridge, Alberta, Can.: Four World's Development Press, University of Lethbridge, 1984), p. 72.

Chapter 4

1. Bopp et al., *The Sacred Tree*, p. 72.

Chapter 5

1. Bopp et al., *The Sacred Tree*, p. 73.

Chapter 6

1. Bopp et al., *The Sacred Tree*, p. 73.

Chapter 7

1. Joseph Epes Brown, *The Sacred Pipe: Black Elk's Account of the Seven Rites of the Oglala Sioux* (New York: Penguin Books, University of Oklahoma Press, 1953), p. 92.
2. Joseph Campbell, *Myths to Live By* (New York: Bantam Books, 1972), p. 63.
3. Matthew Fox, *Original Blessing* (Santa Fe, N.M.: Bear & Company, 1983), p. 176.
4. Tom Brown, Jr., *The Vision* (New York: Berkley Books, 1988), p. 63.
5. *The Treasury of Scripture Knowledge* (London: Samuel Bagster & Sons Ltd., 1969). From the Introduction by R. A. Torrey.
6. Fox, *Original Blessing*, p. 33.
7. Ibid.
8. Ibid., p. 5.
9. Ibid., p. 121.
10. Ibid.
11. Ibid., p. 130.
12. Ibid., p. 176.
13. Amber Wolfe, *In the Shadow of the Shaman* (St. Paul, Minn.: Llewellyn Publications, 1989), p. 317.
14. Joseph Campbell, *Myths to Live By*, p. 72.

Chapter 8

1. Margaret Craven, *I Heard the Owl Call My Name* (New York: Dell Publishing Co., 1973), title page.
2. Lynne Sallot and Tom Peltier, *Bearwalk* (Ontario, Can.: Musson Book Co., 1977), pp. 7–11.
3. Ibid.
4. Ibid.
5. Ernest Wood, *The Seven Rays* (Wheaton, Ill.: A Quest Book, The Theosophical Publishing House, 1925), pp. 62–63.

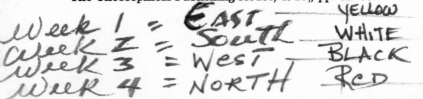